Date Due

BC3 77			
Dec. 24			
Hensall			
MAY 27			
DEC 21			
NOV 13			

FLORA
MACDONALD

by Alvin Armstrong

J.M. Dent & Sons (Canada) Limited

Canadian Cataloguing in Publication Data

Armstrong, Clarence Alvin, 1911-
Flora MacDonald
ISBN 0-460-91698-X
1. MacDonald, Flora.
2. Canada — Politics and government — 1963 — *
I. Title
FC626.M32A75
F1034.3.M32A75
971.06'44'0924
C76-017175-0

ii

Contents

Preface

Canada's Cinderella in politics was born in an obscure town on an island portion of a small Canadian province.

She was reared on thrift and porridge in the Great Depression.

Her heritage, home example, and training gave her self-confidence and fired her with ambition.

In the world of business she battled sex discrimination.

She learned how to travel on a shoestring.

She made the jump from a typist's desk to the male-dominated world of politics.

She became an effective parliamentarian and was encouraged to offer herself for the leadership of the party.

Stumping the country on a limited budget, she convinced thousands of Canadians that she could unite the party and return it to power.

At the polls the delegates faltered, but the public holds her in as high esteem as ever.

She is said to have restored credibility to Canadian politics.

So in losing she wins for all of us.

As a winner she continues to contribute a rare blend of brilliance and common sense to public affairs.

She has become a living demonstration in our own time of what "little people" with stick-to-it-iveness can do for the country they love.

This is the story of Flora MacDonald.

I came upon Miss MacDonald when I began a stint as a staff reporter at the Kingston *Whig-Standard*. She was on the administrative staff of the university in the same city, in the department of political studies, and she was impressing everybody with her charm and political savvy.

Along with my reporting duties, I got caught up in writing a volume on the three hundred years of Kingston's history. By the time I had finished, Flora MacDonald had made her leap into the House of Commons, and political strategists were predicting she would go for the chief prize of leadership.

It seemed to me that the story of this remarkable woman should be told and that the time was ripe. A grant from the Ontario Arts Council helped to provide workers for the project, and so speeded up some items of research, transmission of tapes, and preliminary and final manuscript typing.

For their assistance along the way, my thanks go to Shelly Wilson, Paul Goldstein, Pat Sargeant, Mary Emmerson, Bob Taylor, my wife Wilma and daughter Judiane Brownlee. My thanks too to my colleague Lynn Jones for preliminary copy editing and to J.M. Dent & Sons' editors for innumerable courtesies and professional services.

My debt to Professor George Perlin of the political studies department at Queen's University is immense, for the many hours he gave me in discussing those tides in public affairs which, with disdain or pride, men call politics.

The portrait on the cover jacket is used with the kind permission of Ken Robinson of the Flair Photographic Studio in Kingston, Ontario.

Alvin Armstrong
September, 1976

Part One
Ancestry

1

Parcheesi tonight—or politics?

"Sandy MacDonald's brought one of his girls tonight."

"So I noticed."

"He's not leaving the making of another Tory to chance."

This exchange of remarks at a political meeting in Sydney Mines, Nova Scotia, took place at the back of the miners' hall, out of earshot of Fred MacDonald from nearby North Sydney and his daughter, Flora. The girl was only eleven. It was the year 1937, and this was her first political meeting.

Fred MacDonald, a telegrapher at the Western Union cable office, was a dependable fixture at all meetings in his hometown and some in adjoining towns. Church, lodge, baseball association, cemetery board, or political meeting: coming in for one of these, with snow or the dust of the road on his boots, the stocky Scot with the sandy hair would give a stamp or two of his feet and take a seat near the front.

Mrs. MacDonald accompanied him to many meetings but never to political ones. When Mr. MacDonald and Flora set out this night, Mrs. MacDonald was making over a dress for Jean, the eldest of her family of four girls and a boy. (A fifth girl was born later.)

The young girl had been thrilled at the prospect of going to the meeting, and not just because it got her out of helping with the dishes. Her father had a way of making any outing a mystery crowned with delight, and nights out in the MacDonald household were rare. They were usually on Sunday, and the destination was the church, just a few doors away. A four-mile walk to Sydney Mines had much more attraction than a game of parcheesi.

The second daughter in that MacDonald home was unwittingly making a debut of sorts — entering a field which would eventually become the dominating interest in her life. It was accidental. Her parents knew little formal psychology, so Mr. MacDonald was not saying to himself, "I must stimulate latent interests."

A lifestyle passed on by several generations provided a stable and consistent environment for the MacDonald children. They grew up confident in their surroundings and with a growing confidence in themselves. From their home life and their church alike, they came to know they were loved even when they made mistakes, so they were not afraid to venture.

Flora had already shown an amazing curiosity about everything, whether it walked, swam, flew, or just clung to the underside of a leaf. If it talked — as apparently politicians always did — that would be a bonus.

It would have been hard for her at the time to tell just what it was about the meeting that entranced her. "I was completely fascinated," she said later. "I had never been to meetings other than Sunday School and church, and certainly never to a meeting composed only of men, and here were men all steamed up about things I had either taken for granted or had never heard of."

Having a memory even for nonsense syllables — a fact that delighted her word-grubbing father — Flora saved up some jawbreakers that had been flung around in the meeting. When a neighbour dropped the two off at the door of their Queen Street home, Flora trotted out some of the terms that would later become part of her own stock-in-trade. Right away she wanted an explanation of the "national policy" of her namesake John A. Macdonald (no relation). And she asked about "regional inequities," "imperial preference," "fiscal irresponsibility" and "tariff tinkering." These were the things being talked about in 1937, when people in North Sydney as well as over the rest of Canada were troubled about what was later called the Great Depression.

Soon after this, Flora MacDonald's curiosity led her to "nail" her father about something totally unrelated to her ever-to-be-remembered first political meeting. Up in the MacDonald attic were three mysterious-looking sea chests. Flora's mother used them to hold clothes. In the summer, they held quilts, flannelette sheets, and the children's outer coats; in the winter, summer stuff went into the trunk-like chests. In addition, the chests held a good deal of Mrs. MacDonald's handwork.

4

For the longest time, these three attic chests had been just fancy boxes to Flora, but when she didn't see any like them in her friends' homes, she decided to consult the "home encyclopedia" — her father. What if it should turn out that one of those chests, with its painted-over corner braces, iron bands and lock clasp, had once belonged to that cutthroat pirate, Captain Billy Bones? Maybe at one time it had been filled with "pieces of eight"!

"Your grandfather — my father — was a sea captain," her father explained. "These were the sea chests he took with him when he left home, to be gone for sometimes a year at a time."

Flora and the other children in the home learned at one of their customary evening story times that Grandpa MacDonald had gone to sea when he was only twelve. He had signed on as a cook, no less. He didn't have a sea chest then, probably only a sack his mother had made for him. But he sailed the seas of the world for fifty-two years. And bit by bit, he gathered around him so much gear that he had to put it in sea chests and have somebody take the chests on board ship in a wheelbarrow. Bump, bump, bump the barrow would go, up the cleated gangplank and then along the deck to Captain Ronald MacDonald's cabin.

"I think one of the sea chests was your grandmother's. She sailed with him part of the time."

"What about the MacDonalds farther back?" Flora asked. She knew they had come from Scotland.

2

Out you go—neck and heels!

"Go far enough back," Flora's father said, "and it is plain the Mac-Donalds were not sailors." The children's great-great-grandfather, Donald MacDonald, was born in 1770, in the inland district of Lochaber at the foot of Ben Nevis in the Scottish Highlands. He looked after an estate of some kind, but he may have doubled as a tailor. When he was thirty-five, he married twenty-one-year-old Margaret MacDonald, of another but unrelated MacDonald family. Their first child, Angus, was scarcely a year old when the little family emigrated to Canada.

The transition of a MacDonald family from Scotland to Canada was part of a general shakeup and exodus, called the Highland Clearances, that had taken place gradually after the fateful battle of Culloden Moor, in 1745, when the last resistance of the clans to English rule was broken.[1]

The little girl in the North Sydney home learned that her own name, Flora, as well as that of many a Scottish lass before her, in Scotland as well as Canada, was associated with an emotion-packed incident from those troubled times in the Old Country. The original Flora Macdonald had shielded Charles Edward Stuart — Bonnie Prince Charlie — when he was fleeing Scotland after leading an unsuccessful rebellion against English domination. The prince had escaped, with a reward of thirty thousand pounds posted for his capture, but his enemies were closing in on him. At great risk to herself, the earlier Flora Macdonald had disguised the prince in a woman's clothing and enabled him to make a getaway.[2]

With the suppression of the Scottish clans had come other stern measures, including confiscation of many estates to make way for sheep raising. Dispossessed Highland Scots now looked on themselves as an oppressed people, and family after family left the country. The Donald MacDonalds hung on for some time but cleared out in 1807, probably from the port of Fort William. They left relatives behind.

After a long and frightening crossing of the Atlantic, the couple and their baby were landed at Pictou, Nova Scotia. They remained in crowded Pictou only a few months. Rather than locate permanently in the interior, where the roads as yet were little more than bridle paths,[3] they and other late-arriving Scots took passage on a coastal vessel bound for Cape Breton Island, seventy-five miles to the east.

Sailing through the Strait of Canso, the MacDonalds settled first at a place called River Inhabitants, but they moved later to a coal-mining area, Mabou Mines, near present Mabou. In the years between 1808 and 1825, they added eight more children to their family, including one named Alexander, who would become important in Flora MacDonald's line.

Flora, hearing this story with her three sisters — baby Ronald was only two — was told by her father that she need not be surprised to learn that Alexander MacDonald had become a seaman. Hundreds of Nova Scotia boys, growing up around harbours, gravitated to deep-water ships as easily as boys of today gravitate to cities and start driving cars. Any after-school work young MacDonald was able to find was down at the harbour, three miles away, rather than around the minehead where he lived. The talk around the harbour was much more exciting than that at the mine. It was of yardarms and sails, decks awash with high seas, water-soaked biscuits, far-off ports and an occasional mutiny. So the call of the sea found a ready response in young Alex and he made sailing his life, working his way up eventually to become a mate and then a captain owning his own ship.

In the RED WING Alex MacDonald carried on a coastal trade with cargoes of fish, coal and lumber. Times were good and he did well. He saved enough money to get married, and within six years of his becoming a ship owner he had a small family in his modest home near the harbour.

Then one day tragedy overtook the RED WING. If Captain Alexander had a sea chest, it went to the bottom of the Atlantic with him. His ship was blown out of St. George's Bay, Newfoundland, where he had tried to find shelter from a storm. Ship, crew and captain went down that October day in 1852.[4]

When the father in the little Mabou home didn't return and word got around that he and his ship were presumed lost, it was a sad blow to eight-year-old Ronald. He had occasionally gone on short trips with his father, and on these he had helped the cook, who had taken a liking to him. He had dreamed of going on a trip to the West Indies and of some day, in a ship of his own, seeing Liverpool, Shanghai, Bombay, Melbourne, Buenos Aires and dozens of other port cities.

Despite his father's death he clung to his dream and meanwhile did what he could to earn small amounts to help out with family expenses. He got some work helping ships' cooks while their vessels were in harbour loading cargo. Then one day when he was only twelve, Ronald's chance came, when the cook on a schooner failed to turn up at sailing time. He dared to ask for the job, and the captain, resolving to give the lad help with the cooking, signed the boy on and gave him a berth aft, away from the ship's rougher hands.

Ronald's tote bag was bigger than himself, with everything in it that he and his mother could think of, including two blankets for his straw bed, underwear and socks, a towel, a bar of soap, needles and thread, some writing materials and some rags for bandages. When Ronald later unwrapped the towel, he found his mother's only cookbook.

Young MacDonald began his sea career in 1856, on the leading edge of boom years. The Crimean War had brought a boom in ship construction for the transport of troops and supplies. Every available colonial ship was pressed into service, if not for direct war effort then to fill the gap left by ships diverted to that effort.[5]

The new boy cook looked in on the food stores on his ship: salt beef and pork, potatoes and onions, flour and sugar, dried beans and peas, rice, molasses, tea, coffee, dried biscuits, dried apples and what looked like dried cranberries. He wondered what he would be expected to do with some of the stuff. But with a little help from the captain and the first mate, and in spite of good-natured ribbing from the rest of the crew, he managed.

Twice, however, he brought on the wrath of the volatile captain. Without knowing any better, he washed the dishes in fresh water, which was a precious commodity gathered in casks at ports; salt water would have been good enough. His chores included getting rid of slops by throwing them overboard. Once he threw the ship's cutlery overboard because he didn't see the pieces in the murky dishwater. The crew had to carve wooden spoons to use until they came to port.

Ronald managed in off hours to watch sailors at their work and to read manuals giving ships' terms and descriptions of jobs at sea. He

8

may have burned several pans of biscuits while engrossed in his reading. He went from examination to examination, and from ship to ship, experiencing in the process the sea in all its moods.

"One hand for the vessel and one for yourself!" He learned that early, as he climbed aloft and worked with stiff and flapping canvas while the ship rose and fell and at the same time rolled from side to side. He learned there were times during storms when a sailor doing some necessary work on deck had to lash himself to something fixed and then hang on while a giant sea weighing many tons crashed over the deck and threatened to sweep him overboard. It was then that one took a deep breath and waited to be buried in water. Afterwards, one crept below, hoping to find dry clothes, and all too often found the garments floating in salt water. It was a bad day too when salt water got into the flour and biscuits.

It was no wonder to MacDonald that sailors looked forward to shore leaves. No wonder that most of them got roaring drunk and, being deprived of female companionship, visited the brothels in port cities.

He saw how the hated system of "crimping" and press gangs worked. Unprincipled operators of boarding houses and brothels promised captains they would bring so many bodies aboard, at so much apiece. They got them there by hook or crook — mostly by crook, by getting them as drunk as possible and then feeding them on promises. Some they dragged aboard in a stupor; the men woke up after the anchor was lifted and the shore had receded from sight. They served aboard the ship until they reached the next port — and then did it all over again. It took a determined man to retain his senses as he climbed to mastery of a ship.

Eventually Flora's grandfather made it to the top. Captain Ronald, they called him then. One of the first ships under his command — but not the first he sailed by any means — was the WINNIFRED, of 1,012 tons, built in 1868 at Bear River, Nova Scotia, not far from Yarmouth.[6]

The records available are not clear about whether or not this was the ship the captain commanded when he was married in North Sydney and took his bride to sea with him one August day in 1873. His bride, Eliza Roberts, had come from Ingonish, sixty miles away, and stayed with a cousin until Captain Ronald's ship arrived. After their wedding at the Baptist parsonage in Upper North Sydney, Eliza sailed off with her husband, only a few days before a gale tore twenty-six ships from their moorings in the North Sydney harbour. This was Mrs. MacDonald's first but by no means last taste of a rough sea.

For the next ten years she shared the small living space provided on a ship for the captain. She ate with her husband and the other officers at the captain's table. She darned Captain Ronald's socks, shared his all-too-few leisure hours on ship and shore and perhaps helped aspiring young sailors to prepare for their examinations. Mrs. MacDonald learned that a ship's captain had to be many things. As a businessman he had to purchase necessary supplies, obtain charters, hire crews and manage men for months at sea, often under storm conditions. He had to sell a cargo and arrange for another; pay port taxes; keep an accurate set of books; and see that the ship's log was kept daily. In emergencies he had to be ready to improvise a sail or repair a pump — and occasionally he had to put down a mutiny.

The MacDonald tradition is that Ronald and Eliza's first three children — all boys — were born at sea. The first, born a year after the couple's marriage, was named Alexander after his ill-fated grandfather. The next, born in 1876, was named William Spicer MacDonald, possibly after Captain George Spicer. The third son, Lorne, was born in 1881, on the ship MARQUIS OF LORNE, off the coast of Newfoundland, on a voyage from England to New York. No other woman was on board ship at the time. Whether the birth was particularly difficult (Mrs. MacDonald was thirty-four) or it occurred during a storm is open to conjecture. What is known is that, after naming the boy for the ship and Canada's new Governor-General, the couple decided that if this should ever happen again it would be on land.

So it came about that the last of the captain's children, Flora MacDonald's father, was born on land, in the port of North Sydney, April 4, 1883. Somewhat ahead of the event, Captain MacDonald rented a small house, laid in a stock of food and stove wood, along with furniture, and hoped for the best when he had to sail away. "If it's a boy," he instructed, "I'd like you to call him George Frederick."

Flora MacDonald says this is clearly a reflection of the captain's close friendship with George Murray, long-time Liberal premier of Nova Scotia. Although Captain MacDonald was a political Conservative, he and Premier Murray were on very cordial terms; they entertained each other in their homes, and if the captain happened to be ashore at the time of the annual opening of the legislative session at Halifax, the premier had him there as his guest.

The captain was back in port within six months, to admire his fourth son and to go about finding a larger home for the family. He had local contractors, the Morgan Brothers, build a conventional frame house. The house, with a later enlargement, was to serve the MacDonald family for three generations.

[1] John Prebble, *The Highland Clearances*, p. 145.
[2] In Nova Scotia (New Scotland), not only were some MacDonald children given the name Flora, but some ships too. One vessel was even called the FLORA McDONALD. The Scottish heroine had seized the imagination of Scots wherever they settled.
[3] George Patterson, *History of the County of Pictou, Nova Scotia*, p. 112.
[4] John Parker, *Cape Breton Ships and Men*, p. 169.
[5] F. W. Wallace, *Wooden Ships and Iron Men*, pp. 38, 43.
[6] This ship should not be confused with one of the same name, built in 1905. (National Archives, list of ship registries.)

3
Harnessed lightning

By the time Fred MacDonald, Flora's father, made his entry into the world in 1883, North Sydney was a thriving supply and cargo-loading port, a kind of appendage to Sydney, which is five miles away by crow flight but fifteen miles by road.[1] The town had rather a pleasant situation, sheltered on three sides by wooded hills and on the fourth side having an open view of the sea. The MacDonalds' house overlooked the harbour.

The town had drawn its population from four sources: United Empire Loyalists who had settled after the 1775-1783 War of Independence; Highland Scots — some of the twenty-five thousand who had settled in Cape Breton between 1802 and 1840 (including Fred MacDonald's great-grandfather Donald MacDonald); many Irish settlers who came to Canada following the potato famines of 1845 and 1846; and a large influx from Newfoundland.

Because North Sydney was a port of entry and clearance for shipping, hundreds of ships came there to seek shelter from storms or to drop ballast and pick up a cargo of coal, fish or timber. The ships took on supplies of fresh water, meat, fresh vegetables and a variety of ships' hardware supplies — everything from masts and sail canvas to rope, tackle, stoves, boots and oilskins and hundreds of other items needed on the high seas. For awhile, the port, with its own harbour master, was the fourth in importance in Canada, for tonnage and goods shipped. Only Quebec, Montreal and Halifax ranked ahead of it.

Fred was still at school, in short pants, when the first telephone was installed in the community in 1890. The next year electric lighting came, but probably neither of these conveniences seemed strictly necessary to Fred's mother, however wistfully she may have reported them to the captain picking up her letters in far-off ports. Water service wasn't available for another six years, and a sewer system was delayed until 1902, which meant that Fred MacDonald must have carried water from a pump until he was at least fourteen and used an outhouse until he was at least nineteen.

One of the most significant North Sydney businesses, and the one with which Fred MacDonald would be associated for almost all his career, was the Western Union Telegraph Company, established there in 1875, eight years before Fred MacDonald was born. At its opening it had a staff of twenty-five, consisting of supervisors, telegraphers and supporting workers. The staff was to grow steadily through the years, until during the First World War it would number 325 and the Western Union would have the biggest payroll in the community.

Like most Canadian boys of his generation, and like his brothers ahead of him, Fred took a job as soon as he was out of high school. After an adjustment or two he made it a career. He was first taken into the office of the Canadian Pacific Telegraph Company as a messenger. After a two-year probation period, he received the going rate of five dollars a month and was allowed to find his own way of getting about town. The fact that he could walk to any office or home in North Sydney in ten minutes was an asset.

When he was not delivering messages he was given other chores, and in no time had mastered the Morse Code. The office had no typewriters at that time, so all messages had to be written in longhand. John Bagg, a colleague of those days, says this is one reason Fred MacDonald wrote such a "good hand" throughout his lifetime; it was required for the job and was continued as a habit.

He became so enthusiastic about the code system that he was soon teaching it to some of his friends. But he wasn't long in the CP telegraph office before he seized a chance to move over to the Western Union office, in March of 1901. The staff then numbered about fifty. Young MacDonald began as a cashier and moved up shortly to cable operator, a job he held for the next thirty-seven years.

A 1902 staff photo shows fifty-four male workers and one female — the young woman from the front office. In the photo, Fred MacDonald appears in the very left bottom corner. Even at nineteen his facial features are the striking image of his daughter Flora at the same age. People in North Sydney today who knew the MacDonalds after Fred became a family man remark on the resemblance.

During the years when Fred's mother was raising her sons in that North Sydney home, Captain Ronald was sailing from port to port in leaky windjammers. He was being buffeted by more than waves. Wooden vessels were now having to compete with steamdriven vessels with iron and, later, steel hulls. The freight market was tough. The old carriers of the Atlantic trade were being driven to distant seas with low-class freights. Insurance rates on wooden ships were high, especially when inevitably the ships were dropped below A-1 classification, following routine inspection of their leaky hulls.

Some voyages had to be made in ballast, because no cargo could be obtained in a given port. Sailing these old windbags became a losing game, so much so that for at least one trip, and probably for others, MacDonald signed on a coal-carrying steamer as first mate.

By 1885, the end of the wooden sailing vessel was in sight, but Captain MacDonald hung on. During the 1890s Canadian owners of wooden hulls powered by sails got rid of their vessels as fast as they could, because these ships were no longer money-makers. So a large number of captains and mates of the old school were left without ships.[2] The youngest of them went into steam. But many captains who knew nothing but square-rigged sailing, and didn't fancy becoming junior officers, retired to farms. Still, Captain Ronald hung on. The last ship to come under his command was the MUSKOKA, a four-masted barque built in England in 1891. For very good reason she was known as a great cargo vessel. She could carry over 2,000 tons and carry it fast.

Back in North Sydney, the captain's now white-haired lady had done more than her bit in raising her family. Alex left home at fifteen and later matriculated at Dalhousie University. After working in a law office in Halifax, he worked for newspapers in Boston, New York and London, England. He joined the Black Watch Regiment and served in the South African War and then in India, Burma and China. He was far from home; his mother had no need to stay there for him.[3] Lorne, when he finished school, had worked for a photographer in the hometown, but he died of blood poisoning at eighteen. Five years had passed since his death. William, called Will, had gone to work in the United States.

Only Fred was left, but he was now twenty-one and well able to look after himself. Having completed his high schooling, he had gone to

The Queen
Street house

Fred MacDonald
as a young man

work in communications. By now he was well established, but apparently a convinced bachelor.

With encouragement in one of the captain's letters, Mrs. MacDonald said goodbye to Fred and crossed the continent by train to join her husband and his ship at the far side of the United States. She sailed then in the MUSKOKA, with a cargo of lumber bound for Chile. After a long delay there, the square-rigger was off again, bound for a port in Germany.

It had been years since the captain's lady had experienced the terrors of a passage around Cape Horn: the penetrating cold, wind shrieking in the rigging, gear creaking and groaning, seas crashing overboard. It must have seemed like another childbirth. For two years, 1904 to 1906, she followed the sea, dreaming of retirement for the captain and a life together on land, back in the North Sydney home. Meanwhile she hooked a great square rug for what was to be the captain's cosy den. The dream came true, and the captain's sea chest was trucked to the Queen Street home and placed alongside that of his lady.

After fifty-two years at sea and still in good health, Captain Ronald looked around for a job on shore. At age sixty-seven, he was appointed harbour master at North Sydney. About this time, Mrs. MacDonald's sister, Susan Roper, having lost her husband David, gave up the boarding house she was running at Glace Bay and moved in with the MacDonalds and their son Fred.

[1] Full details on North Sydney may be found in a brief unpublished history by Fred MacDonald and a volume published by Elva E. Jackson, entitled *Windows on the Past*.

[2] Wallace, *op. cit.*, p. 321.

[3] Later, he rejoined the Black Watch for service in the 1914-1918 war, first in France and then in Persia. He was killed in action, Jan. 21, 1916, in the Battle of Essin, on the Tigris River in Mesopotamia.

4
Not a bad idea!

When the First World War broke out in 1914, Fred MacDonald was thirty-one and still single. Younger men were enlisting by the dozen, and the temptation must have been strong to join them. But the cable station, with an increasing volume of urgent business, was considered indispensable to the war effort; a telegraph key was as important as a rifle or bayonet. The cable station was under constant guard against sabotage.

To cope with expanding business, the station moved to much larger quarters in a new building in Court Street before 1914 was out. By then, the all-male staff, except for a girl in the front office, numbered 122. But because men were in short supply, a number of other girls were added to the staff.

Meanwhile, Fred MacDonald, who couldn't get overseas with some of his friends, used his annual holiday to take short trips to such places as Bermuda and New York. He was fond of operatic concerts and of professional baseball. His favourite big-league team was the New York Giants. MacDonald made friends easily and was no recluse by any means. The pay at that time for a cable operator was about $25 a week, so he couldn't travel as often as he might have liked.

One of the girls added to the station in November 1918 was to bring a new dimension to his life and, as things were to work out, to Canadian political life. Mary Isobel Royle was born in Newfoundland but brought up in North Sydney.[1] She wasn't quite sixteen when she joined the staff, and soon she was operating a special telegraph machine called a Multiplex.

17

Molly, as her friends called her, completely won the heart of the now thirty-five-year-old MacDonald. By that time he had the marks of a rather well-established gentleman. Molly saw him as a man of character, respectful rather than bold, a churchman but at the same time a man of the world, knowledgeable in public affairs — a fun-loving but solid type.

Molly's arrival on staff could not have been better timed as far as Fred's routine life was concerned. His parents were getting on in years, and so was his aunt; if Fred didn't get a hustle on he would soon have to go back to doing his own housekeeping. That conviction wasn't arrived at suddenly, but it grew on him as he dated this young woman, recognized as one of the prettiest and best-mannered girls in the North Sydney community.

Captain MacDonald died soon after Fred started dating Molly, and two years later Mrs. MacDonald died also. Aunt Sue kept house for Fred, but she too passed on, in 1922. Fred MacDonald's comfortable little bachelor world had been shattered. He was ready for marriage, and when he talked it over with Molly Royle, he was able to convince her that it was not a bad idea at all. They discussed his interest in baseball and the Masonic lodge. He already knew she shared his interest in church.

The two declared their vows in the Methodist parsonage on July 5, 1922, while rain came down in buckets outside. He was thirty-nine and she was nineteen. After a brief honeymoon at Margaree Forks, sixty miles away, the couple took over the MacDonald home. The house would be considered a fair size today; for awhile the two must have rattled around in it.

The new Mrs. MacDonald found that one of the three sea chests in the attic contained a number of ships' flags, including Canadian flags and flags of various other countries. There were numerous signal flags, predating ship telephones. The couple concluded that the Canadian flags must have been rescued, one by one, for sentimental reasons, when the captain's ships were sold from under him to foreign owners who would have no use for a Canadian flag. By the time the captain was through with the sea, he had a fine collection of these trophies.

---

[1] She was the only remaining child of William P. Royle, of Altrincham, England, and Julia Earle, of St. John's. The couple's first child, Jack, died at age six. Mary was the second child. A third, Mildred, died at two months.

Part Two
Childhood and Youth

5
Molly put the kettle on

"It's a boy, Molly! Won't Fred be proud?" The doctor held the baby up where the mother and the midwife could see it.

The twenty-year-old mother insisted the baby be named after his father. With Frederick settled on, and a little toying around with middle names, the parents agreed to pick up the name Lorne, which had fallen out of the family with the untimely death of Fred MacDonald's older brother.

"Lorne would be forty-two now," said the baby's father, as he made a mental calculation. "I think he would have been pleased to know his name would be continued." It was not to be continued for long; little Lorne would die before he was four.

Meanwhile, the Fred MacDonalds "balanced the family" when Lorne was fourteen months old. The parents called the second child Jean Mary. Molly, whose real name was Mary, wouldn't consent to that as a first name, but she agreed to it as a second name. "Jean goes so well with Mary," she said.

A year and a half after Jean's arrival came Flora Isobel MacDonald, who was later to enter Canadian politics. She came howling into the world on June 3, 1926, with dampened wisps of hair a little redder than gold. In time, political wags and journalists, seeing that hair, now beautifully coiffured, and being aware of the social concern in its possessor, would call Flora the Red Tory.

Curiously enough, on a very depressing day many years earlier, a British prime minister, Spencer Perceval, a religious fanatic if there ever was one, had predicted that the world would end in 1926.[1] For Flora, it was just beginning.

The Sydney *Post* marked the child's birth by a comment in the personal column, in which the MacDonald name was misspelled:

Mr. and Mrs. Fred McDonald, Queen Street, are receiving the congratulations of their friends on the birth of a daughter this morning.

The same newspaper noted that King George V's birthday, the same day, was being quietly celebrated.

The movie notice for the Palace Theatre advertised *The Sky Raider* — based on the Great Train Robbery of 1903. In the sporting world, Babe Ruth hit two home runs that day, to give the Yankees "an easy victory" (8-5) over the Boston Red Sox.

In London, England, Lloyd George, Liberal party leader, was given a vote of confidence following a denunciation by Lord Oxford. In another distant part of the world, Los Angeles, the spectacular woman evangelist, Aimee Semple McPherson, was being held captive for a $25,000 ransom; there were suspicions that it was a hoax.

Nearer home, in Canada's capital Dr. George Vincent, president of the Rockefeller Foundation, in addressing a nurses' gathering, deplored the fact that Canada was "sending some of her best brains to the United States." A brief editorial in the *Post*, quoting the St. Catharines (Ontario) *Standard*, bewailed the general exodus of job seekers to the USA, and blamed the Mackenzie King government. The baby born that day in North Sydney would grow up and make the same point, except that she would blame one of King's successors, Pierre Elliott Trudeau.

Flora was given her mother's middle name (Isobel) and baptized at St. Matthew-Wesley United Church by Rev. John S. Sutherland. She didn't remember that, of course. She was later to say that her first memory of Dr. Sutherland was that she had to face him in his living room and apologize for throwing a stone through his kitchen window. "That wretched stone," she said, "not only broke the window but a bottle of milk on the window sill."

By that time, Flora had lost her brother, but she and Jean had been joined by three sisters: Helen, Ruth and Sheila. Ruth lived only three years. With three remaining little girls in her care (Jean 6, Flora 5, Helen 4) and new baby Sheila, Mrs. MacDonald had her hands full.

She was fortunate in getting daytime help, at the going rate of about a dollar a day, from a succession of neighbour girls. The helper would come in at eight in the morning and leave about the same time at night, when Mr. MacDonald was around to help with the chores.

Mrs. MacDonald had additional help, especially at intervals when no teen-age helper from the neighbourhood could be enlisted. Mrs. Wilcox Spracklin, who had reared Molly MacDonald from childhood, spent a good deal of time in the MacDonald household. "She was our adopted grandmother," Flora said later. And apparently the affection the household had for Mrs. Spracklin was returned.

Mrs. Spracklin says that when Flora was about six, the little girl and a playmate came over to "Grandma" Spracklin's place and managed to kill a toad in the Spracklin garden. "Believe me, I gave them a good talking to," she said.

Another North Sydney neighbour, Miss Emma Lewis, tells of having three of the MacDonald girls, in turn, in her kindergarten class. The day the school flag flew at half mast to recognize the death of Robert Stanfield's father, Frank Stanfield, Lieutenant-Governor of Nova Scotia, Miss Lewis tried to explain that "the man who looked after the country" was dead. Flora MacDonald's explanation at home was just a trifle different: "The man who looks after Miss Lewis's field is dead."

The MacDonald household, like all others in North Sydney and the nearby communities — indeed in all of Canada — felt the effects of the Great Depression. Fred MacDonald had steady work at the telegraph centre, but his earnings, while better than those of day labourers, were still small. All members of the family can remember having handed-down or made-over clothes.

"One of my favourite recollections," said another neighbour, recalling Flora MacDonald's childhood, "is of seeing her in a kilt of the MacDonald tartan, with a black velvet jacket, and a Scotch bonnet perched on her auburn curls — truly a bonny Scots lassie. That costume was all the work of her mother's hands, expertly tailored and perfect in every detail."[2]

Mrs. MacDonald, when she wasn't washing, cooking and baking, was cutting and sewing, basting and darning. One wonders where she got time to bake and do fancy work for church suppers and sales, but somehow she did. And when, as occasionally happened, a new minister's family moved into the manse next door, it was to find preserves and fresh home baking in the cupboard waiting for them.

A great deal has been made in magazine articles of the influence of Flora's father. Without intending to detract from the equally strong influence of her mother, writers have by their omissions tended to do exactly that, which is a disservice. The mother in that home, by her gentleness, Christian faith, practical wisdom, infinite patience and impartiality, left her own life-long imprint on the lives she brought into the world. Wherever the children went in later years, they were frequently overtaken with a yearning to see "Mum," and they gravitated to her across thousands of miles.

[1] Lucille Iremonger, *The Fiery Chariot: A Study of British Prime Ministers and the Search for Love*, p. 48.
[2] Miss Jennie Hackett, letter to the author. Flora says if she had curls they were created by her mother; her hair is naturally straight.

6
The Pied Piper

Wherever there are school teachers there is gossip about their pupils. Miss Lewis said that one day she asked her principal about the MacDonald children, "How is it they're so clever?"

"How can they help it with a father like Fred MacDonald?" he said. Every teacher in that school knew what he meant. MacDonald was indeed a rare person, the kind a community never exactly duplicates. He had an inquiring mind, and like the Athenians among the Greeks, he had enough leisure to enable him to put it to use. His daily job at the telegraph centre left him his evenings, Saturday afternoons and Sundays.

He was devoted to his family, his church, his lodge and other community organizations, and had the knack of being able to parcel out his free time so as to serve them all. To the four girls coming along in the home, who were like stair steps in height — Jean, Flora, Helen and Sheila — Mr. MacDonald was tutor, recreational director and tour guide, all rolled into one friendly package.[1]

"Look it up!" he would say, again and again, when he was asked how to spell a word or locate a fact. He was a dictionary man and a researcher of sorts himself. He spent a good deal of time in his own den, as well as in the "reserved" section of the local library. He wasn't much of a borrower at the circulation desk. Except for reference works, if he considered a book worthwhile, he bought it. He was a bear on pronunciation and syntax, and often tackled the local preacher for misplaced accents and modifiers.

25

Flora, Helen and Jea

Flora and Helen

Helen and Flora
in Scottish dress

Left to right: Ronald,
Helen, Jean, Flora
and Sheila

Tutor MacDonald knew the value of incentive. To get homework cleaned up in a hurry (but it had to pass inspection), he read to the children every week night when they were young. He might also read to them Sunday nights. "We not only had the children's classics read to us — books like *The Swiss Family Robinson, Kidnapped* and *Uncle Tom's Cabin* — but the adult classics as well," Flora recalls.

The lives of the storybook people were real to her. The repeated reading experiences became an emotional as well as rational foundation for her later concern for all classes — the so-called populist quality in her character. Into the core of empathy built up around the family dining-room table were built later experiences in her hometown and elsewhere in her ever-expanding world.

Saturday afternoons were reserved for outings. A neighbour says that from the time the girls were out of the cradle they could be seen somewhere with their dad, if the weather was at all pleasant — even sometimes when it wasn't pleasant. He might have the baby in her carriage, or have one of the little ones perched on his shoulders. The others would be strung out behind. Frequently the group would cluster while Dad would explain something of interest — anything from a species of bug or toad to the operations of a ditchdigging crew.

As the children grew older, Mr. MacDonald took them farther afield and let them bring chums from outside the family. Jean says: "I would have a couple of my friends along, Flora would have Ethel Patterson, and Sheila would have Flora Patterson. Because there were two Floras, the "short one," who was the new minister's daughter, was called "Little Flora.""

Mr. MacDonald was referred to as the Pied Piper because he often had such a troop following him. One Saturday, the group would be off for a picnic; another day, for a swim; another, for a rare train ride or, rarer still, a trip on one of the vessels that called at North Sydney and plied up the coast and back.

On one unforgettable day the expanded MacDonald clan was taken for a short sail on the famous Nova Scotia fishing schooner, the BLUENOSE.[2] The talk that day between Fred MacDonald and skipper Angus Walters was rather evenly divided between the schooner's racing performances and the seagoing exploits of Fred MacDonald's father, Captain Ronald.

Like most Cape Bretoners, Fred MacDonald was keenly interested in sports. As the children grew too old to be read to, he took them to baseball and softball games. "Father always took two or three season's passes at the ball park at Sydney Mines [four miles away]. There were

28

always two or three of us children who walked there and back with him," Flora said. No wonder her dad, when he wasn't called the Pied Piper, was called Baseball MacDonald.

The Second World War broke out when Flora was thirteen and in high school. The war put a damper on field sports for men; there just weren't enough men around for a team on the old sand lots, although service men at the sea, army and air bases had their own teams.

High school was a "must" for Flora, as it had been for her father. The extra input her father had made for all the little MacDonalds during their elementary years, in opening their minds and giving them a facility in language, seemed to give Flora, at least, a zest for knowledge beyond her years. She had pegs now on which to hang an ever-expanding world of ideas.

But she had her spells of rebellion too. When she was only twelve she got her back up over the Shorter Catechism, or at least the Shorter Catechism as it was being thrown at her in chunks in church membership classes. She thought she should understand the document, point by point; but the minister seemed content to have the class memorize the questions and responses and was impatient with Flora for wanting it all broken down into plain prose.

When she took her complaint to her father, he gave her a choice: either she would memorize the catechism or, as an alternative, memorize an equivalent number of selected passages from the Bible. Flora chose the latter and, later, as an adult, said she was sure she made the right choice. She was not against the catechism as such, but her teachers remembered that even in kindergarten she wanted to understand everything that was being presented to her.

By this time, a drive to succeed, for which Flora MacDonald has been known ever since, had taken full hold. One is not surprised to have one of her fellow classmates say: "Flora was something of a tomboy — as keen on sports as any of the boys at school, but when it came to schoolwork she was sharp. She was old when she was young. It made it difficult for the other girls to compete."[3]

She won a provincial cup one year for submitting the best essay among Nova Scotia children on the subject of fire prevention. She was prominent as well in fund-raising events and in school plays. In addition she found still other things to do. The 1941 issue of the school yearbook presents her as the assistant editor. The next year — her final year — she was editor-in-chief. She included in the issue an original and fairly lengthy poem entitled "The Sons of Canada" — dealing with Canada's armed forces in training and in the front lines.

Flora, Helen, Jean
and Ronald

Grade VIII girls, 1938-39.
Flora is third from the
left in the second row.

Eleventh grade class.
Flora is at the
centre of the picture.

Flora rests during
a May 24th hike.

The poem shows a maturity beyond the writer's fifteen years.

During this same period, Flora belonged to the Canadian Girls in Training (CGIT). At one of the annual candlelight vesper services she unwittingly singed the hair of the girl ahead of her; Flora was gawking at the effect of hundreds of candles lighting the church auditorium.

In the CGIT organization she made her debut in public speaking and her debut as well in outdoor camping. Years later she could recall the agony of her first case of homesickness, but she remembered as well the rush the girls made for the dining room at mealtimes, and to the sports field; the frenzied activities the girls engaged in to make sure their tents were ready for inspection; and, not least, "muted conversations through the night when spruce bough mattresses proved less than conducive to sleep."

As she grew older she graduated to the church's older youth group. The young people put on their own plays, in addition to the ones they helped put on at Central High School. At least one of these was repeated at the army base. The personnel there gave the MacDonald girl a standing ovation for her handling of the female lead role.

Identification with her church youth group made her eligible for the annual camping session at New Campbellton on the Bras d'Or Lakes; she wouldn't have missed this for all the chocolates at Carmichael's Store, and one of the youths who shared in these camp outings said Flora was "in the middle of all the camp pranks too."

A teen-ager like this, bubbling with energy and going all out at church and school, could be called neither a religious kill-joy nor an academic drudge. The student who wrote the customary yearbook tribute to Flora as a member of the 1942 graduating class — one of those pieces they call school "obits" — represented Flora as saying, as she left high school behind:

> Happy go lucky, fair and free,
> Nothing there is that bothers me.

---

[1] Later, in 1934, a son, Ronald Alexander, was added, and still another girl, Lorna Ruth, in 1940, when Flora was fourteen.

[2] The famous ship was launched five years before Flora MacDonald was born, and until Flora was thirteen, the schooner from Lunenburg was often seen tied up in various Nova Scotia harbours, including North Sydney. After a period of service in the West Indies, the "Queen of the North Atlantic," as she had been affectionately called, sank near Haiti. The schooner was later "replaced" (but not duplicated in all respects) by BLUENOSE II.

[3] Kenneth Boyce, interview.

7

When a bump is a boost

The end of Flora's high schooling at Grade 11 (which was the equivalent of Grade 12 in some of the other provinces) was a crisis bigger than the sixteen-year-old girl realized at the time. The step she was forced into by circumstances at that time was to determine, or at least condition, much of her future.

Had she gone on at once, scholastically, as some of her classmates did, although their grades were behind hers, she might have added an academic degree or two to her name. But, inevitably, as the university system functions, she would either have stopped with a generalist grounding, represented by a BA, or acquired an MA or PhD specialty which would have channelled her into one compartment, where she might have been stuck for life — possibly as a teacher.

As it was, she was to gain a working tool, in secretarial science, which would serve her through any number of careers, making her less dependent on office secretaries — or more sympathetic if and when she came to use their help. And she was to gain a broader education through travel and discussion than could have been gained by exposures in a university ghetto of classrooms, libraries and extracurricular activities.

Flora would get to a university later, but meanwhile her father's relative poverty and North Sydney's limited job field steered her in another direction.

It wasn't a happy girl who set out by bus for the Empire Business College at Sydney, fifteen miles away. She said later: "This was the one time when I really questioned my father's direction in my life. I

33

wanted to go on to university, but in Cape Breton at the time it was just not feasible, except for the daughters of well-to-do people."

She could train as a nurse, or go to normal school and become a teacher, or go to business college and then into an office. Those were the three options. There were no others. There was no way, at that time, to get a government grant for university training. And there was no such thing as a summer job that would pay a girl enough money to underwrite university. The parents, with a family of six, could see no way to send her.

If anyone were to go to university from the MacDonald family, as subsequently happened, it would be Flora's brother Ronald. He got there by going to work for a couple of years first. That was the way the educational process was regarded in North Sydney in 1942.[1]

Flora says, "While I wanted to go the university route, and inwardly felt that if my dad had really wanted me to go he could have found some way to get there, I was told it wasn't possible. I accepted it, although with a heavy heart, and decided to go to business college."

It will be no surprise to learn that this teen-ager didn't enjoy her year at business college, or that, according to her standards of perfection, she didn't do well there. Her heart wasn't in it. Typing and shorthand were mechanical things, which one could whip up with half a mind. There was no challenge.

It was only later that the girl was able to reassess that year. All her later work, until she became a politician (and even then) leaned on the skills she acquired that year. She learned enough shorthand and typing to be able to go into almost any office and set herself up as a secretary. She could hire on for short periods, as her financial needs dictated, and then move on to follow a yen for travel. It would be her way of bankrolling her way around the world.

She still uses the skills she acquired in that year at the business college. But she says she will never forget the chagrin of riding back and forth on the bus with many of her old classmates of Grade 11 who were now taking Grade 12 in Sydney, before they went on to university. She who had led the class in the upper grades in North Sydney was going to a trade school! The daily ride seemed to rub in the distinction that was being made. Maybe the others were coming to feel she really was inferior! It infuriated her.

But there were a couple of compensations that helped to relieve the bad taste of that year. Ruth LeMoine, one of Flora's best friends from Grade 11, was in exactly the same situation. Their shared misery cemented their friendship.

34

The other compensation was that she and Ruth loved to ice-skate, and Sydney had an indoor arena. The girls often slipped over to the rink after business-school hours. This meant hitch-hiking home or being driven home by one or another of the girls' skating partners, such as Kenneth Boyce.

Boyce, who now works in the Sydney television station, doesn't claim to have been rated more than anyone else as a special boyfriend. "Flora had many friends, and I don't think any of us counted more than others," he said. (Flora agrees.) But Boyce is enthusiastic about Flora's skating ability. Along with everyone in their skating crowd, Flora had speed skates, and when she hit the ice with a long graceful stride learned from her sports-loving father, she attracted the better skaters among the men and boys as her skating partners. She would skate the whole evening, letting up for only long enough to thank one partner and take on another or for the ice scraping that went on at half time.

Flora MacDonald still turns up now and then at the Sydney rink, and now that her own town has a closed rink, she skates at the Forum there on any of her brief winter visits home. (Her mother still lives in North Sydney.) When Flora appears on the ice, a dozen of her old partners will shout their greetings from the bleachers or come swooping in for some fast turns around the rink. If she appears in Sydney, it's nothing for one or more burly steelworkers from Whitney Pier to swoop in and take her for a few flying rounds.

According to Kenneth Boyce, "When Flora gets out there on the ice, you can see the tail of her short coat streaming out behind. Her hair is flying and she's in another world." When the evening is over Kenneth and his wife Blanche will have the MP over to their house for hot chocolate.

Flora and her friend Ruth finished their business course together, and both offered themselves to the business community. Flora says she was as nervous as a cat in her first personal appearances and tryouts. At the air base she was rejected out of hand. "I'm sure I was not what they were looking for," she said. She suspects today that her dad, who knew almost everyone in town, had something to do with her getting on as a junior clerk at the local branch of the Bank of Nova Scotia. Arrangements were made for her to begin at the end of the summer. Meanwhile, Flora and a friend who was visiting her decided to have their own kind of holiday.

[1] Ronald worked his way through Mount Allison University (BA and B. Ed. degrees).

8
Go slowly — you'll see more

Today the spectacular Cabot Trail, which goes almost to the tip of Cape Breton, is being strongly promoted by Nova Scotia's tourist industry, and the roads branch of government has co-operated nicely. Visitors to the province can wheel around the 184 miles of ever-changing landscape in a few hours; and the faster they go, the less they see.

Flora MacDonald walked about a hundred of those miles before taking up her job in the Bank of Nova Scotia. The road wasn't paved then, and in places it hadn't even been widened.

Flora suggested the idea to her friend Ethel Patterson, of the same age, who had come to spend a few summer weeks with the Mac-Donalds. Ethel, it may be remembered, was the daughter of the former minister. The two girls had been close chums until the Patterson family had moved away the previous winter. At that time the girls had promised to keep in touch and to get together in their summer vacation.

"That's great — absolutely terrific!" Ethel said, when Flora sprang the idea. Flora had already talked it over with her father, and he had agreed in principle, although there were some details he wanted to work out if Ethel consented to go.

Flora had been around the trail several years before, with her father and Dr. J. S. Munro, on one of the doctor's occasional trips to visit his patients. His scattered practice extended from Margaree clear to the tip of the island. The road had been a one-way affair and a challenge to the doctor's car. The track wound up and around, and up

36

again, through deeply wooded hills. When they emerged on the east side of the cape it was to find themselves hundreds of feet above the Atlantic.

"It's like nothing you've ever seen before, or ever read about!" Flora told her friend. And she explained that since her first trip, changes had been made. A vast acreage of forest near the tip of the cape had been declared a national park (1939), and the road had been widened in places. But it was still a gravel road. "You won't want to walk it in your dancing shoes," Flora said.

Dad got into the picture at this juncture. He insisted that walking the whole length of the trail was unnecessary — "unless you want to set up a new hiking record." The girls would see the same kind of country on both sides of the cape. "The east side is more spectacular."

He proposed that they take the coast boat, the ASPY, to Dingwall, or to Pleasant Bay, well around the tip of the cape, and then walk back. Mr. MacDonald would use his contacts with other cable operators and retired operators, at intervals along the east side of the trail. It was hoped that each would provide accommodation for a day or so, and when the girls were ready for the trail again, the last host would recommend them to a friend or relative in the next village or somewhere along the road. They could make their way home at little or no expense, and they would need little gear.

Arrangements being made, the girls set out on the ASPY. Their knapsacks held a change of clothes, rainwear, a change of footwear, a water canteen, a first aid kit for possible blisters, and some mosquito oil. Both girls had trekked before with the CGIT.

Flora had been on the vessel before and had the satisfaction now of showing her friend around. Once out of the North Sydney harbour and beyond the point at Sydney Mines, there was nothing but water to starboard. Flopping onto a bench, Ethel said, "I'd like to sail on and on until we come to England." Flora confided that "one day and on a different ship — maybe out of Halifax, or Pictou, or Saint John, or Montreal, or even New York — who knows? — I'm going to get to England."

When the ASPY had made several stops to drop supplies at coastal ports, the girls prepared to disembark at Dingwall, near the tip of the cape. For the past hour, off the port side, they had observed a seemingly unending shoreline of ragged bluffs, crowned with forest. Here and there they had seen a ribbon of road at the cliff's edge, and they knew that they would be following that perilous track on the way back. Clutching the rail on the upper deck, Flora and Ethel had watched long breakers hurl themselves against the rock face and fall again into the sea, as if stunned. Now and then a breaker, hitting an outcropping at an angle, would run along the oblique face, sending a spume high in the air.

Backpacks in place, the girls came down the gangplank and were met by one of the Angus MacKinnon men from five miles up the road. "I knew you must be them by your packs," he said, and led the way up a narrow winding road to the upper plateau.

From there the girls turned to look back. The ASPY was still being unloaded. Beyond the wharf where the vessel was tied was a fishing dock and a pocket of inner harbour where fishing craft of all kinds were closely anchored. Here and there a lone fisherman was splitting cod on the top of a post that rose from the timber framing of the dock. Beyond the masts of the fishing fleet and the funnels and deck-rigging of the ASPY, no land could be seen — only whitecaps glowing in the sun.

"That's Sugarloaf Mountain," their guide explained as he led the girls past some scattered houses nestled at the base of another almost sheer cliff face. "They say it's only 1,800 feet high," remarked Flora. "The Rockies are higher — but it makes you feel kind of insignificant." She was already feeling the therapeutic effect of the holiday. Sydney's Empire Business College was a nightmare to be forgotten. The benefits it conferred — if any — would come later.

The girls had no intention of spending more than a night at the MacKinnons', but the family would have "none of this running off again when you're barely past the door." So the telegrapher's daughter and the minister's daughter, with little experience of farm life, tried to get the knack of picking up a forkful of hay without standing on it and to master the art of milking.

The girls' five senses were pleasantly assailed day and night. Sunrise over the Atlantic, with no land mass like that out from Sydney to get in its way; sunsets, when a ball of fire dropped into the forest on the cap of the mountain; jagged pines silhouetted against drifting clouds; the sounds of gentle rain on the cottage roof, of swallows chuckling under the eaves of the barn; the tinkle of a sheep bell just before one dropped off to sleep; the smell of blueberry muffins; the taste of buttermilk fresh from the churn.

All too soon the two had to express their thanks and hit the road, but not before hearing a Gaelic blessing:

> May your road rise with you;
> May the wind blow always at your back;
> May the good Lord hold you in the hollow of His hand.

Down, down, down, the road descended, winding back and forth and coming frighteningly close to the edge of cliffs — so close that the girls kept to the inside of the gravel road, except for the times they got up courage to stand at the edge and look down to where waves were smashing themselves to death below.

The two passed through the fishing village at South Harbour. A dozen miles later, footsore and dust-covered, they were received by the John Alex MacLeods at Neil Harbour.

"We went from family to family, until after a couple of days we reached Ingonish," Flora said. She had relatives there. Her grandmother, Eliza Jackson, had come from Ingonish to North Sydney exactly seventy years before to marry Captain Ronald MacDonald. Ingonish was still thick with Jacksons. There were so many of them, in fact, that the girls couldn't decide just where to stay. On a toss-up they stayed overnight with friends at an inn.

The ASPY, coming up from North Sydney, brought Flora's father and her nine-year-old brother, who had decided to come that far and walk the rest of the way back with the girls — still a matter of sixty miles. Mr. MacDonald was then sixty years old, but his legs were as good as ever, he said.

Leaving Dad and young Ronald for a day in Ingonish, the girls climbed through rugged bush to the highest lookout point in Nova Scotia. Following an overnight rest, they were off again with Mr. MacDonald and the boy.

Perhaps the most exciting part of the trek from Ingonish south was the walk over Cape Smoky, which is 1,500 feet high and juts out into the Atlantic. The foursome stopped with farmers or at lodges which provided bed and breakfast. The latter places were run by former telegraph operators, so Mr. MacDonald knew them all.

Evenings were spent in spinning yarns and re-telling political stories. "The entire experience was tremendous," Flora said. "You could just let your imagination run wild."

All too soon the party was back in North Sydney. Time would blot out some of the inconsequential details, but appreciation for Cape Breton's grandeur would remain. And the experience of hiking the Cabot Trail would encourage Flora to believe she could use shank's mare again, as she would in Britain and on the Continent.

9

Don't blot that ledger!

In 1943, even more than now, a bank's general premises tended to overawe the youth of a community. A massive high counter and a caged teller, as well as the still-familiar vault, inner rooms, secret ledgers, a manager in the background, the common notion that there were signal buttons everywhere (connected with the police department) and an awareness that the commodity dealt with made the whole world "tick" gave many people an indefinable feeling of reverence the second they passed the threshold.

Flora MacDonald felt all this on Thursday, August 12, when she asked at the counter for Mr. Schurman.[1] The manager released the counter catch and led her to the back of the room. Flora was conscious of half a dozen pairs of eyes following.

She was relieved to greet another Macdonald she knew — a pleasant woman who shared the same surname but with a different spelling. "I'm the small 'd' Macdonald around here, and you'll meet Charlie over there who is a 'Mc' and not a 'Mac,' " she said. This concentration of clan folk wasn't really surprising. Cape Breton, including the Sydneys, is still full of MacDonalds, Macdonalds and McDonalds; the latest telephone directory has 174 of them in North Sydney and Sydney Mines alone.

Genevieve Macdonald set Flora MacDonald to work copying what were then called collection drafts into a big ledger.[2] The copying had to be done with a steel-nib pen, which was then the universal tool in Canadian banks. The ballpoint pen was coming into general use and would eventually replace both the fountain pen with its internal ink-well and the steel nib that had to be dipped. But the ballpoint's use was forbidden by most bank managers for fear its ink would fade.

Flora hadn't used a straight pen since she had had to do writing exercises with one in early school grades. It terrified her to have to use one now, in case she would create a horrible blot in the ledger. Somehow she managed, by making shallow and frequent dips in the inkwell, to keep from blotting the massive book.

Early in the assigned chore, the manager came around and looked over the new junior's shoulder. He explained how important it was to make each figure distinct, so a three couldn't possibly be mistaken for a five or an unfinished eight, and a seven couldn't be mistaken for a one or a sloppy nine. To make sure she got the point, Mr. Schurman had her do some figures while he looked on. Flora was to find that, between jobs, a junior had to practice good penmanship in general. It was like being back in Grade 4.

Other first-day chores were assigned. In fact, when Flora had survived the initial day she went tripping home to report that she had already had a promotion. "I was allowed to count money!" she announced, which amazed and even alarmed her father. This was going altogether too fast, even for a brilliant daughter; he must speak to Mr. Schurman about this. "No, I'm not a teller yet, but I've been counting and wrapping pennies and nickels," she said.

Starting pay was $40 a month. The junior clerk started paying board at home, which was customary for all young people in her culture when they had jobs and lived at home. She started her own bank account and salted away as much as she could of each pay.

Helen MacLean, who came to the branch two years after Flora, described Flora as an A-1 worker, popular with the staff, conscientious and completely reliable. In her six years in the branch, her ability was recognized as she worked up from junior clerk to ledger keeper, to teller, to assistant in the loan department and eventually to assistant accountant.

Promotion was slow for female employees. Flora discovered this early in her banking experience. Miss Gennie had been in the branch for years; eventually her title became "acting accountant," and her pay was in keeping with that designation, but she was doing the work of an accountant and had all the responsibilities of that position. Not only that, in practice she was virtually the manager. Customers would come to her with their questions, rather than to Mr. Schurman. So would other staff. So would inspectors and auditors.

Flora knew that Miss Gennie resented the injustice, and Flora herself was inwardly furious. Her feelings had nothing to do with the women's liberation movement, which, as such, hadn't surfaced yet. To Flora it was just a plain piece of injustice in the banking system that anyone, man or woman, could be required to do a "higher" job and be kept in a "lower" category to save bank costs. If a woman was in effect the bank manager she should be called the manager, never mind the silly tradition that banks had only males as managers. She was to find abundant opportunity further along the line to express herself on women's rights in a male-dominated world. And when she would, her recollections of her first job would come flooding back to her.

Her feeling about inequities in bank pay for women came out indirectly in a little experience at the end of a day well along in her career in the North Sydney bank. She had hurried out of the bank at closing time, bound for some outdoor adventure. She discovered that she had left her handbag behind. A bank employee admitted her when he heard her rattling the door, and she explained her reappearance. As the employee let her out again he said, "You can't go far without your money, can you?"

"No — but you can't go far with it!" was the rejoinder.

The Second World War was now over and changes were taking place in the MacDonald household. Mr. MacDonald had retired in 1938, at age fifty-five, because changes in the telegraph system called for a reduction in staff. While he was one of the last to go, he had been encouraged to take an early pension. But with the outbreak of the war a year later, communications took on new importance. The staff was increased, and Fred MacDonald was brought back for the war period, this time as a censor who had the codes to all war messages.

Now with the war over, he retired for the second time, at sixty-two. He had plenty of time now to read more in the five newspapers to which he subscribed, to research and write concise histories of his church, his lodge and the community in general, to act as secretary for the cemetery board and take a prominent part in promoting baseball, as well as attend many of the games.

The MacDonald home was a comfortable place, but Flora began to wonder if she shouldn't make a move. She had gone as far as she could in the local bank and she began to hanker for a wider experience of her world. Her sisters, Jean, Helen and Sheila, had all left home to take work in other cities, leaving only Ronald, 15, and Lorna,

8. Many of Flora's close friends had either married or moved or both. Flora was twenty-three. She had better get a move on.

She had kept in close touch with her friend Ethel in Peterborough, Ontario. Ethel had graduated from Queen's University and was working with the Children's Aid Society. When Flora told her of her feelings about making a move, Ethel invited her to come and seek work in Peterborough and share her apartment.

Flora got a transfer to the bank of Nova Scotia in Ethel's city, ninety miles from Toronto, and off she went. She had often been away from home before, but only for short visits. This was to be a major break with North Sydney and 156 Queen Street.

Her father had already developed his own way of keeping in touch with his girls. When Jean, the eldest, left for Montreal, her dad wrote her a weekly letter, describing everything that was going on around home. When Helen left, he added a carbon copy for her, and a second carbon when Sheila left. Now he added a third carbon. The letters have been part of the family treasure ever since, along with the senior MacDonald's daily diaries.

In Peterborough the girls shared an apartment and went out daily to their respective jobs. In after hours they threw themselves into the same cultural events. They sang in a church choir and joined a community choir as well. Both choirs put on performances, and some of these were taken to communities outside the city. The girls greatly expanded their circle of friends.

Before long, however, Flora was offered a promotion to the staff department of the bank's head office in Toronto. Difficult as it was to interrupt a variety of associations in Peterborough, she took the Toronto job. She was obviously searching for something which she herself would not have been able to define.

Settling in with a Scottish family of Finlaysons, who had moved to Toronto from North Sydney, Flora went through the now familiar pattern of linking up with a church and a performing choir.

But when the first summer came around (1951) she told her employers that staying in Toronto for a summer was more than a civilized person should be asked to bear. She was going to have a little holiday at her Cape Breton home. To make it easy for the bank, she quit; but she promised to return in the fall. She kept the promise, and the bank was happy to have her back.

That winter something happened in England that made Flora MacDonald's feet itch again. An event that was half serious and half a lark stirred the Scottish part of her to the depths. A group of students from Glasgow University had gone to Westminster Abbey in London, swiped the famed Stone of Scone from under the Coronation Chair, and taken it back to Scotland where they were sure it rightfully belonged.

Talking about this later, Flora's eyes lit up and she became eloquent. "To me that was the most imaginative, romantic, and daring thing that had been done in my lifetime. To think that somebody had actually tackled this — upset the whole of Scotland Yard, the Royal Family, the Government of Great Britain. Three or four students were able to disrupt the establishment. It wasn't a malicious thing. There was nothing mean or petty about it. It was somehow daring; it had a large element of risk. But these students actually believed that this stone meant a great deal to the history and tradition and culture of Scotland — that its rightful place was in Scotland."

The event so stirred Flora MacDonald's imagination that she thought to herself, "I want to meet the students." From that moment on she decided she must go to the United Kingdom — not just to meet the perpetrators of a deed that warmed a Scottish heart three thousand miles away, but to get to know the Old Country, from which her Highland ancestor Donald MacDonald had come.

[1] G. M. Schurman was manager 1939-1946.
[2] When cheques became more common, collection drafts tended to drop out of the picture in banking.

Part Three
Work and Travel

10

The orchestra was lousy

Anyone following the movements of the MacDonalds in the summer of 1952 might well have wondered what they were up to. Flora and her mother left for England within a day of each other, on different vessels. But on the spur of the moment, one had to take one's bookings where one could get them. Flora sailed from Quebec on the RMS SCYTHIA, July 7, and her mother from Halifax the next day on the NOVA SCOTIA. Flora landed at Southampton and Mrs. MacDonald at Liverpool.

The daughter had managed to persuade a fellow bank worker, Doreen Holroyd, whose home was in Blackpool, England, to accompany her on the journey. Then the Finlaysons, with whom Flora lived in Toronto (a family with roots in Nairn, Scotland) came up with an idea — doubtless with some persuasion from their eighteen-year-old son Ralph — to add Ralph to the party, provided the girls were willing to take him along.

The girls had no reason to object. So for the next few weeks Flora and Ralph, to prepare themselves for hitch-hiking in the Old Country, did a few trial hitches out of Toronto, to Montreal and elsewhere. They went on long hikes and even climbed the Scarborough bluffs to get themselves in condition.

Flora set out with a one-way ticket, a hundred dollars and the confidence she could find work to pay her way back. The threesome on the SCYTHIA had a pleasant crossing. This was not only because the Atlantic was well behaved, but because the trio, even before reaching the port of Quebec, fell in with a group of young musicians going to the Continent.

The groups merged, in varying combinations, on the ship's deck and in the dining room and lounges. The ship's orchestra was no great shakes, but the young people tried to dance to it anyway. Rudy Toth, the talented pianist, entertained at several impromptu concerts, at the urging of the passengers and the entertainment director. The second night out, the group stayed up until morning to see the sun rise. The ship was in the Strait of Belle Isle at the time, and the rays of early light falling on icebergs in the vicinity made a spectacular show.

The three Continent-bound youths prepared to take their leave at Le Havre, and Flora and Doreen skipped another night's sleep, intending to wave them off at three in the morning. As it happened, the customs officials didn't clear passengers until 6 o'clock. Flora admits that when officials weren't looking, she went ashore for a minute, just to be able to persuade herself she had been on French soil.

At Southampton, their own port of leave, the original threesome decided to find a hotel, get a night's sleep — since they had missed one — and get an early start to London the next morning. Five hotels insisted they had no rooms, so the good-hearted taxi driver took the three to his place, where he and his wife put them up in their prefab cottage for the night.

The taxi driver's wife brought hot tea to her guests' bedsides in the morning. This, followed by a breakfast of bacon and eggs, which probably used up some of the family's precious coupons,[1] was the first but by no means the last touch of hospitality the Canadians would receive during their time in the United Kingdom.

Deferring their hitch-hiking for the time being, the group took a train into London. Flora and Ralph helped Doreen find her train to Blackpool, and then the two set out to see what they could of central London, including Trafalgar Square and the Soho region. Meeting up with other friends from the ship, they did the rounds of Hyde Park, the Marble Arch, Westminster Abbey, the Houses of Parliament, Big Ben and even Buckingham Palace. At the palace gate, Flora talked at length with a bobby. "He let me try on his helmet," she told her travel diary.

The two took rooms at a reasonable hotel, and the next morning, by tube and bus, they got themselves a good distance outside the city and tried their first hitch-hiking. They were setting out for Altrincham, in Cheshire about 180 miles north, where they expected to find Flora's mother visiting relatives in her ancestral village.

The two knights of the road wasted that first morning going in a wrong direction, but an obliging young man drove them back all the way and got them headed right before he went his own way. This was more unexpected hospitality.

The visitors were impressed with the villages and towns they passed through as they rode in a succession of cars and lorries. But Flora couldn't refrain from commenting on what seemed an excessive number of chimneys on most houses. "What a country for chimney sweeps!" she remarked to Ralph. She was impressed too with the distances they seemed to be covering. This was one of the adjustments she had to make after the vast spaces in Canada.

They passed Winston Churchill's birthplace, Blenheim Palace, crossed rolling meadows and entered Stratford-on-Avon. They considered themselves fortunate in getting tickets for an evening performance at the Great Memorial Theatre. They went out and found cheap lodging for later, returned to the theatre and waited for the curtain to go up. The play was Ben Jonson's *Volpone* — not what they would have chosen, but its scathing yet mockingly humorous exposure of human greed found sympathy in Flora, with her plain and thrifty background. She was in the homeland not just on a lark but for an education. This play would be the first of dozens she would see in the next seventeen months.

Another driver picked up the pair the next morning and later waited for them while they did a quick turn around Warwick Castle. Yet another ride took them as far as Coventry. Here they visited the great cathedral and took a side glance at Lady Godiva's statue. The hitch-hikers were in Leicester for supper with "friends of friends" back home. Wherever Flora goes she carries an address book and she is continually adding to it.

These friends entertained the pair overnight. The next morning they drove them through Sherwood Forest and later took them to an English pub — an old place with wooden beams, where women as well as men were quaffing beer.

Reaching Altrincham later that day, Flora found her mother had made a good sea crossing and was being well entertained. The next day was Sunday. The house guests, Mrs. MacDonald, Flora and Ralph, were taken by bus to Llandudno in North Wales, a distance of only sixty miles. Again, Flora was struck by the compressed nature of the Old Country. At this rate she would be able to scoot around the entire island in short order.

This is exactly what she did before going back to London and looking for work. She had resolved to make the first weeks holiday weeks and then look for employment.

During the next few days, she and Ralph hitched their way across the Scottish border, over the Douglas Moors, along Loch Lomond, across the Moors of Rannock and westward to the Isle of Skye. This was the island from which the original Flora Macdonald had come. The Canadian Flora was losing no time tracing this historical root.

On the ferry from the mainland, while she was in conversation with the captain, she gave her name. The skipper chuckled in disbelief and said, "Call me Bonnie Prince Charlie!"

On her second day on the island, she found the Scottish heroine's grave in an old cemetery on the western side of the island, and noted the epitaph, in the words of Samuel Johnson: "Her name shall be mentioned in history, and, if courage and fidelity be virtues, mentioned with honour."

Flora found the island all that her reading had led her to believe. Modern ways had scarcely touched the place. The sabbath was strictly observed, but the natives had an equal reverence for whisky. One old lady, it was said, always said grace before she had her daily glass — straight. An old man told the visitors, probably with a twinkle in his eye, that in making his morning porridge he used whisky instead of water.

During this turn around Scotland, Flora didn't catch up to the students who had snatched the Stone of Scone, but she did get to the Ambroath Abbey, where the Glasgow culprits had hidden the stone before it was discovered and taken back to Westminster. She also visited the War Memorial at Edinburgh and found that it bears the names of all members of British regiments who gave their lives for their country. Flora discovered there the name and record of her father's eldest brother. The entry under the heading *Imperial Black Watch* reads thus: "MacDonald, Alexander, born Halifax, Canada, S/8444, Sgt., killed in action, Persian Gulf, 21.1.16, 2nd Btn."

Flora and Ralph, after darting around Scotland for three weeks (during which time Ralph had time to look up his relatives around Nairn), were joined by Doreen, and the three took off for London, Dover, the English Channel and Paris. They spent six days around the French capital, visiting much publicized spots, including the Flower Market, Notre Dame Cathedral and the Eiffel Tower. They put up each night at a hostel. A side trip took them to Versailles.

Returning toward England, they recrossed the Channel at Dieppe. The crossing was so rough that many people were seasick, including Flora.

The compression of this narrative may convey the notion that this dashing to and fro was very superficial. On the contrary, a reading of Flora's travel diary and her letters home indicates that prior to visiting each historical scene, she read up on it at length. She took literature with her, and at each place she asked endless questions and made careful entries in her notebooks.

Her own careful education in the North Sydney home, by a Scot with a deep love for the homeland, gave Flora an abundant set of pegs on which to hang her own impressions. Considering also her remarkable memory, she is possibly one of the best informed short-term visitors to both Scotland and England. Her brief trip as far as Paris, however, was only an appetizer for a later eight-week visit on the Continent.

Back in the United Kingdom, Flora and Doreen attended the Braemar Festival of Highland games and did some more tripping around the country. Then Flora considered the vacation portion of her homeland visit ended. After another stopover at Altrincham she prepared to return to London and look for a job.

---

[1] A rationing system introduced during the Second World War, and using coupons, was continued for some food items for several years afterward.

11
Who's for tennis?

Mrs. MacDonald went to London with her daughter. Flora had learned of a man who made regular trips from Altrincham to London, and she got his consent to take the two women with him. It was the nearest Mrs. MacDonald ever came to hitch-hiking — a practice she frowned on, but about which she had learned to keep her peace.

They made London in four hours, in a new Bentley, and the two put up at a YWCA, on a Saturday night. Sunday morning they went to a nearby church, but to their dismay, after they were seated, they discovered it was a Welsh congregation and they couldn't understand a word. Flora faked a cough and got them out.

Beginning with a "Y" contact, Flora tracked down a rooming place, and her mother helped her move her things there. She was going to be able to get her own meals, which would be cheaper than boarding. But it was an hour and a quarter's run into the heart of the city. She decided she would have to make the best of that for awhile, but she did hate wasting time on the road.

Then Flora fell into conversation at Canada House with a Canadian girl, Elaine Barber, who was living in the St. John's Wood district, in the west end. Elaine, originally from Winnipeg, had a McGill University degree and was engaged in research. She invited Flora to move in with her and share expenses. It would cost them about three pounds each per week, plus their food and bus fare, and they were only fifteen minutes by bus from central London. The apartment consisted of two large nicely furnished rooms — a living room and bedroom with twin beds — and a kitchenette and bathroom. So much for a place to stay. Now, to get a job.

Flora and her
friends have seats for
the coronation parade .

After seeing her mother off for Halifax, Flora began her search for work. She found the going tougher than she had expected. Writing to her father after several weeks, she said, "Work hasn't been easy to get. Last week I had some pretty blue days when I thought I would have to go on the dole. The moment you say you are a Canadian, employers back away. They find 'colonials' don't stay too long. They want good stenographers and my shorthand isn't fast enough now to step into such a position cold."

She nearly walked her feet off, applying at offices and stores in central London. But in the end she landed a job as an appendage of sorts to Selfridge's, Limited — one of the largest and most popular department stores in London.

The store had a staff of over two thousand. The management operated a social and sports club, complete with a beautiful club house, for the benefit of the staff, on a membership-fee basis. The full-time secretary in charge of club operations had just left when Flora appeared, asking for work. She got the job.

She described it to her father as an "assistant's position" — having to do with arranging for sports like badminton, tennis, hockey, swimming, archery, cricket and football — just the thing, he must have thought, for a sports-minded girl. The job also involved arranging dances and other social get-togethers, and the boss wanted to see square dancing added to the recreational offerings. Flora would also be in charge of handling membership finances, bills for food and other services.

Two fringe benefits meant that Flora had a free membership and a store discount. Unknown to her at the time was the fact that the experience she would gain in steering so many people and events would help prepare her for organizational work in a political context when she would return to Canada.

From that initial contact forward, Flora MacDonald was a going concern around the Selfridge Club and apparently was considered highly satisfactory to the management. In the course of her duties, she was taken to dinners and plays by several office and store executives. One even took her across London on the back of his motorbike to a boat race, in which Cambridge easily defeated Oxford. On weekends Flora made short trips out from London.

Elaine Barber was expecting to be shifted to Paris and so she gave Flora three weeks' notice of the possibility of a move. Flora persuaded Dorothy Chisholm, a Canadian nurse she had met on board ship and again in London, to move with her to an apartment at 4 Burwood

Place, on Edgeware Road. The apartment wasn't up to the quality of the earlier one, but it was cheaper and only five minutes from Flora's work.

The coronation of Queen Elizabeth II, in June, brought an invitation to Flora and two girl friends to occupy three reserved seats along the Mall and to attend a gala garden party within the grounds of Buckingham Palace. The girls felt elated over that. "Apparently we're in good standing at Canada House," Flora remarked in a letter home.

Following the event, she had this additional comment: "How often I've stood at the gates of Buckingham Palace, my nose flattened against the bars, and wondered what it was like on the other side." She let her dad know that inside those walls she and her friends, in their best frocks, had talked with Canada's Liberal Prime Minister Louis St. Laurent and the leader of the Progressive Conservative Party, George Drew.

From the sublime to the ridiculous, she might have said a few weeks later, after quitting her job at Selfridge's. She and Dorothy took a job as farm labourers for fifteen shillings a day. They wanted an outdoor job and were anxious to round out their experience, as well as to get in physical condition for an autumn tour of the Continent. The place was Salford Priors Farm, in the Midlands. The first week there, the girls picked black currants, and then they were given a hoeing job for five days. Their muscles ached, and intermittent showers left them damp and mud-spattered.

"We've had the last two weeks on our knees, and at the same time we've been trying to separate one fragile little sugar-beet from fifty of its kind, and still leave it standing. Our rows looked like collapsed lines of toy soldiers, when we finished," Flora told her home folk.

After working in the fields all day, the girls would clean up, as best they could with cold water, and sometimes hitch-hike to Stratford, where they would get standing-room-only tickets to a performance. They took in five performances under such conditions.

Later, some of Flora's political associates would wonder where the woman got her stamina. "In the beet fields of England!" would be her usual answer.

12
The House of Bohuntin

When Flora went overseas, she went armed with information from her father about her ancestors in the Lochaber district in the Highlands. She was determined to root around at the first opportunity, to see what else she could learn.

Having to depend on pick-up rides rather than being able to command her own transportation, she often had to make a quick choice about whether to continue with a long ride or get out of a car part-way and make a trek off the beaten track. On her first trip into northwest Scotland she and Ralph had come within hailing distance of Fort William, but for the sake of getting all the way to the Isle of Skye she had bypassed her ancestor Donald MacDonald's former district, roughly twenty miles from Fort William.

Later, on a weekend spent in hitch-hiking in Perthshire with Dorothy, the golden opportunity presented itself, beginning with a chance conversation in a store. A Charles MacDonald, who was also interested in putting together some of the pieces of information he had obtained about the clan members in the Lochaber district, got just enough of Flora's story to set him on the right track in finding the place they were both looking for.

Setting out in the MacDonald car, the sleuths located the hamlet of Bohuntin (now spelled Bohuntine) up a dead-end road on the side of a lovely glen in the wilds of Lochaber. All around them as they made their way along a narrow dirt road were towering mountains, with the peak of mighty Ben Nevis rising above them all.

In the hamlet of Bohuntin were perhaps half a dozen cottages. The three in the car got out and began to make inquiries about the remaining MacDonalds in the area. A young man informed them that everybody in the hamlet was a MacDonald! But on learning who the visitors were, he led them off to visit his father and mother.

The old couple were "real highlanders," according to Flora. The relative, several generations removed, of the Donald MacDonald who had left there in 1807 was also named Donald MacDonald. He had never been far from his home glen, but was full of knowledge of the MacDonald line. Crippled with arthritis, but standing and leaning on two canes, he expounded the history of the House of Bohuntin. It was obvious to Flora that at crucial points the story not only matched, but amplified, the story her father had told her: the Donald MacDonald who had left there a century and a half before had been known as the "tailor of Lochaber."

The narrator's little old wife insisted that the visitors have a wee bite, and she brought out homemade bannock and shortbread, which she served with tea. The old man went on with his story. Just that spring, he said, their large home had burned to the ground. With feeling, he told how his library of over a thousand books, many of them out of print, had been destroyed. The old couple was now living in a tiny croft nearby.

As she stood there listening to this wizened old scholar, Flora understood in a flash how the Highland passion for learning had somehow been passed on, generation after generation. She knew little, so far, about any academic prowess the Donald MacDonald who had gone to Cape Breton may have had or about what his sons had done to carry on the tradition. But she knew that a great thirst for knowledge, not just of books but of the ways of men, had possessed her grandfather, Captain Ronald MacDonald. And her father, Fred MacDonald, back in North Sydney, had been painted with the same brush.

She recognized this thirst in herself too. It was part of the reason she was now in Britain. She was satisfying an indefinable passion to learn — anything, everything, for whatever use it might have. As she had moved among people — in the Sydneys, in Peterborough, in Toronto, and now in the Old Country — she had learned that some persons have this "something" and some haven't. She had it. She hoped she would never lose the thirst.

Glancing around from the doorway of the little cottage, Flora could see the ruins of the old crofts from which her ancestors had set out.

The migration of her great-great-grandfather from this hamlet at the foot of Ben Nevis to the New World had eventually provided her with an opportunity to contribute her bit to the Canada that had been in their dreams. What she would make of that opportunity, she was not yet sure.

Before the visitors left, the old lady went upstairs and changed to her good dress; she and old Donald hobbled out into the yard so they could have their pictures taken.

Riding out the narrow and twisted road, Flora wondered how her ancestor, the earlier Donald MacDonald, his wife Margaret and their little son Angus had made their way out this trail and over the trackless twenty miles or so that they would have taken as the nearest way to the port of Fort William — and ultimately to Canada.

13
The bull hasn't a chance

Our Great Continental Tour, Flora called it in anticipation, when she and Dorothy were toiling up a mountain near Llanrwst in North Wales, in the summer of '53. The girls had been planning to wind up their sojourn in England in the spring and take eight summer weeks hitch-hiking on the Continent before returning to Canada. But they had been persuaded to avoid travelling in Spain and Italy in the heat of summer. So they worked on farms throughout Scotland and waited for time to pass.

The berry farm was the most primitive situation they had encountered since deciding to work in the great outdoors. They lived in a makeshift wooden hut, with no warm water and no electricity, and slept on straw beds. They had planned to stay two weeks but had arrived late in the picking season. They toughed it for ten days, collected their shillings and looked for another casual job. They got one that rather terrified them. It involved beating the bushes in highland country to scare out grouse for hunters, who seemed to insist on shooting from all directions.

Catching a ride into Aberdeen, the girls found a "Y" where they were able to wash up and wash their clothes. They had to admit they looked very grubby. Once, along the way, they had been picked up by the driver of a cement truck. He said he guessed his outfit wouldn't make them any dirtier.

Hurrying now to London, they had their passports checked and went as far as Canterbury for the weekend, to get an early start on Monday, September 14. The channel crossing was smooth enough,

Keevil farm camp, Wiltshire, 1953

The MacDonalds of Bohuntin

Costa Nova,
Portugal, 1953

St. John's Newfoundland. Auntie Mab
and Mrs. Spracklin welcome Flora back to Canada.

but hitch-hiking southward in the general direction of Paris was painfully slow, compared with getting around in Britain. They were only fifty miles out of Calais when they had to put up for the night at a hostel — a dirty one with communal washrooms.

The two girls were foot-slogging mile after mile the next day when they got a four-hour ride to Paris with a pair of young Brethren missionaries — a four-hour ride and a four-hour sermon. Having seen Paris the year before, they pressed on to Chartres, Tours and Bordeaux. In the last-named they stayed overnight at a convent recommended by some fellow travellers.

They got almost to the Spanish border when a tropical hurricane lashed their hostel at Biarritz. Whiling away the time with other trekkers brought to mind again the old proverb: "Misery loves company." But while the winds and rain tore at the building, the travellers shared their experiences of the road and told about their homelands.

"Our final twenty-five miles in France (before crossing the Spanish border) were worth the other six hundred as far as scenery was concerned, and if ever I return for a holiday to France it will be to the colourful Basque coast, preferably one of the little fishing villages. The lovely stretches of golden sand, the huge waves from the aftermath of the storm, the blue mountains and blue seas, and the clusters of small fishing craft with their hulls and sails of bright yellow, red or blue, have left a vivid picture with me," Flora wrote to her home folks.

Crossing into Spain created no border problems, but the two found distinct changes in life style. Houses were of adobe. Most older women were dressed in black, but younger women were dressed in gay colours. A French driver took hairpin bends at a fast clip, leaving Flora and Dorothy gasping as they looked out over a sheer drop on the outside of the road.

When they were most despairing of another ride, along would come another Good Samaritan and whisk them off, usually in the back seat. The last miles to Madrid were in a chauffeur-driven limousine, from which the hitch-hikers descended to seek a cheap room. They spent the next three days walking about the streets; they found them half deserted by day but full of gaiety every night.

At Salamanca, near the Portuguese border, two very dejected girls sat and sat and sat, and then walked and walked and walked, through village after village. In one village they were mistaken for pilgrims on their way to Fatima, near Lisbon; people came out and offered them bread and wine to refresh them and wished them well on their way. They needed the cheering up. "Some pilgrims!" Flora chuckled, as she produced her trusty jackknife and opened the blade. She hadn't used the weapon, but it was reassuring to know it was handy. Dorothy, the nurse, had a long hatpin concealed in her shoulder bag.

Still short of Lisbon, in grape country, they stopped to see four men in bare feet tramping grapes in a huge tub. "I hope they washed their feet," Dorothy commented. "Not at all; it helps the flavour!" was the superintendent's rejoinder.

Back into Spain at Seville, they had an opportunity to see their first, and last, bullfight. They left after half an hour of what Flora called "barbaric torture, the bloodiest, cruellest excuse for sport that I ever hope to witness. The bull doesn't stand the slightest chance."

Leaving the poverty of southern Spain behind, the two returned to Madrid and then took roads leading northeast. Eventually, they were picked up and driven to the French border by a very personable young man. One can imagine his passengers' chagrin when he was arrested for stealing the car and the girls were arrested as accomplices. It took some explaining to get out of that.

Cold and wet, the girls in their now threadbare jackets, wrinkled skirts and sodden sandals tried to avoid the stares of the idle rich along the French Riviera. They were on the road to Rome, determined to make it at all costs. And the cost in discomfort now was high. The rains were upon them and the nights were cold. At Genoa they wondered whether Christopher Columbus, who had set out from there, had ever been as cold.

Earlier, in their travels through Spain, Dorothy had reacted in the night to a meal that had too much bull fat and too many snails. Now after a restaurant meal somewhere between Pisa and Rome, it was Flora's turn. "Bad fish!" she said between spasms of retching.

Rome at last. Vatican City, St. Peter's Cathedral, the Sistine Chapel, the Museum and the Coliseum made up for a lot of the unpleasant experiences they had had in getting there. And Rome was the turning point for dear old Blighty and home. "We should be back in England in two weeks time," Flora announced, after consulting maps.

Florence and Milan detained them for a view of historic sites. And then Switzerland was their host for a couple of days. "The grandeur, majesty and beauty of Switzerland were overpowering, and we could only gaze in silence, knowing that any words we could utter would be most inadequate," wrote Flora in one of her letters home. She indicated that she and Dorothy would not be long in England once they got there. They were anxious to return to Canada.

It was now the 25th of October. How well they knew it when they got out of a car in the St. Gotthard Pass, at 6,800 feet, in ankle socks and flimsy skirts and gazed down through a whirling snowstorm!

At Baden-Baden in Germany they caught up with North Sydney friends who were stationed there with the Royal Canadian Air Force. Then it was Cologne, Frankfurt, and out of Germany into Belgium, through Belgium to Brussels and then to Ostend and the coast.

Again they crossed to England, and again they hitch-hiked into London, another seventy miles. A warm bath at the "Y", and they were ready to collect their mail at a former rooming house, gather up some warmer clothes, and in order to raise enough money to get back to Canada, look again for temporary work. Earning enough in waitress work and other casual jobs delayed their departure. In off hours, Flora attended sessions of the British House of Commons.

Only days before turning up at Liverpool to catch their ship for Halifax, Flora MacDonald was madly typing a manuscript for a Daphne du Maurier book, *Mary Anne*, the biography of du Maurier's great-grandmother. Her trunks and Dorothy's had gone ahead to the ship. Another Canadian friend, Connie Savage, who was going to Canada with them, had arranged to meet the two on board.

They had left London so often in the past seventeen months that it was hard for them to believe their farewells this time would be for good. Flora declares she arrived at the ship with sixteen pieces of hand baggage, and Dorothy had almost as many. "When we get to Halifax we'll need a van," Flora said.

They arrived home on the NOVA SCOTIA on December 9. And somehow they got their luggage shovelled into a night train leaving for Sydney and North Sydney.

"What did your trip to the Old Country do for you?" Flora was asked later. She said: "It gave me an assurance I needed, that I could make my living under almost any circumstance . . . that I could handle myself in any given situation . . . that it wasn't a demeaning thing to do any kind of honest work. I saw how people in various circumstances coped with those circumstances. Their example will always be with me."

14

Sandals in a horse trough

Two months after returning from the United Kingdom Flora took an office position with a textile firm in Montreal. Her sister Jean was married and living in that city. Flora moved into an apartment on Claremont Avenue and was joined there that fall by Dorothy and Connie, both of whom had previously held nursing positions in London and then Halifax. Dorothy and Flora had already become well acquainted in their trekking together in Britain and on the Continent, and Connie proved to be just as compatible. The nurses worked at different Montreal hospitals, and their shifts weren't always the same, but when time off coincided, the congenial threesome did many things together.

As usual, Flora flung herself into a busy round of activities. She attended a United Church and usually made it to the morning service as well as a Sunday evening club which featured lectures on a variety of subjects.

Monday was her regular night for badminton at a Presbyterian church hall, and she often played on Thursday nights as well. This was an old game to her and she became good enough at it to take part in a friendly tournament against some Chinese students at McGill University. She excelled in volleyball as well. After a regular evening of play it was not unusual for her to walk two miles home to save bus fare.

Fridays she attended classes in Scottish folk dancing at the "Y". On other nights, unless she chose to stay in and read, there were opportunities for dinners out, movies, plays, concerts, debates, and at widely spaced intervals, house parties with a group of Scottish friends who were also working in Montreal. She confesses that on at least two such party nights the group made such a racket with their singing of Scottish ballads and their dancing that the neighbours in the flat below complained.

On the political side, she took part as a canvasser for Egan Chambers in the November 1954 by-election in the St. Antoine-Westmount riding. In the two winters she was in Montreal she became an enthusiastic weekend skier, usually at the YM-YW camp at Christieville in the Laurentians.

Correspondence related to Flora's Montreal experiences reflects a remarkable breadth of interest, all the way from romping with her little nephew Donald and giving Donald's mother a break so she could have a night out, to serious discussion about political policy for the country as a whole. A Burns Night was a must, but so was going to hear a visiting choir from the Toronto Bible College.

Work at W. R. Brock and Company Limited involved her in a variety of office procedures, including shorthand and typing, as well as the use of several office machines. Much of it was routine. While she earned a name for efficiency and never complained about scrapping a social engagement to push through an added piece of work, there was little about the job that called for her ability to be creative. When she had been there a year, she told her father in one of her letters that she saw no future in continuing at Brock's, "so I would say a move is just about due."

Dorothy and Connie had no ties in Montreal, and as nurses, they were used to moving around "for experience." So with a second summer in the city coming up, the three planned to head for the far west and seek, if not their fortunes, a change of scenery. In their travels in Britain and on the Continent, Flora and Dorothy had been asked many questions about their own country that they hadn't been able to answer. Flora, in particular, felt a keen thirst for a knowledge based on experience, such as she had had in Britain and on the Continent, and not just on classroom teaching and outside reading.

At first the girls planned to leave their Montreal jobs at the end of April, 1955, head south to New York and Washington, then west to Calgary, arriving there toward the end of June. They thought of seeking some casual work there and taking in the Stampede before proceeding to Vancouver for permanent work. They revised the plan slightly: they would continue in Montreal to the end of May and so eliminate the need to seek work in Calgary.

They had notified the landlord of their intention to move out at the end of April, so they decided to shift in three directions for the final month in Montreal. Flora would stay with Jean and her husband Emory; Dorothy and Connie would stay with relatives or friends.

Flora knew her father would frown on her making so many changes in her career. She told him, half in fun, that she intended to keep on the move until she had seen the Taj Mahal in India and "swum in the pool out in front"; then she would be happy "to settle down in some out-of-the-way village."

The Brock people were so complimentary of her work and so reluctant to see her go that Flora began to have second thoughts about pulling out of Montreal. She had also gathered a large circle of friends and hated to leave them.

"Now that my time is running out in Montreal," she wrote, "I begin to wonder if I'm doing the right thing to be pushing on again and leaving all the good times and the pleasant-enough setup which I've carved here. But no sooner do I think along these lines than Tennyson's words come to mind — 'Yet all experience is an arch wherethro' gleams that untravell'd world, whose margin fades for ever and for ever when I move.' Perhaps I should stop, but something within me would be terribly unsatisfied, and I shall just go on, horizon-chasing."

No one could understand better than Flora MacDonald the almost companion lines of Kipling:

> . . . a voice, as bad as Conscience rings interminable changes
> On one everlasting Whisper, day and night repeated — so:
> Something hidden. Go and find it. Go and look behind
> the Ranges —
> Something lost behind the Ranges. Lost and waiting for you. Go!

Flora preferred to hitch-hike west. "It's much more exciting," she argued. But the other two talked her into combining finances and buying a cheap car. "We'll be independent and be able to go where we want to," Dorothy argued. At the moment she was the only one of the three who could drive, but she was willing to do it if the others would put in their share for the capital cost and expenses along the way.

For the next few weeks the girls and a couple of their men friends looked over the choices on the used-car lots, to see what could be picked up for about $300. A salesman who had a soft spot in his heart for Dorothy offered them a 1946 Chevrolet for $200. Adding insurance, registration and a couple of tires, they were still within the figure they had estimated, so they closed the deal.

Dorothy drove the car home — and stalled it on a streetcar track. With the streetcar motorman clanking his bell and motorists honking, the girls sat looking down at their toes. Men rushed at them from all sides and pushed them around a corner. A slight wait while the motor unflooded itself, and they were on their way again.

The last day of May saw the trio head out of Montreal in the direction of New York, Dorothy at the wheel, Flora beside her as navigator, and Connie crammed in with an overflow of luggage in the back seat.

The car performed well in New York, Washington and Williamsburg, allowing the Canadian visitors to give attention to American politics and history. It took them safely to the door of Flora's Uncle Will in Greensburg, Pennsylvania. This now-oldest brother of Fred MacDonald trotted out his research of the family tree and said he had gone back to 125 A.D. He'd have gone back to Noah, he said, but he "didn't have room on the paper."

The old car brought the tourists briefly back into Canada at Buffalo-Fort Erie and later sat uncomplaining while they took in the breathtaking beauty of nearby Niagara Falls at night, under everchanging coloured floodlights. Again, Flora's relatives — this time sisters Sheila in Toronto and Helen in Rochester, Minnesota — provided not only convenient stopping places but a chance for Flora to catch up on recent family history.

The need for new brake linings at Rochester brought a howl from three thrifty girls, who hated to hand out an unexpected $45, but fortunately Flora's sister Helen had married a doctor, who was on a post-graduate fellowship at the Mayo Clinic. "No problem," he said. "We're paying $25 a pint these days for blood. Just get in the lineup in the morning and you'll have your brake linings for nothing and have some cash left over."

"Blood-letting day!" Dr. Moffitt shouted the next morning before he set out for the clinic. The man was as good as his word, and soon the three donors were on their way west, through South Dakota, Wyoming and Montana.

At a park in Montana, three Canadian girls, having breakfasted as usual on oatmeal porridge, noted that the day was an American holiday — July 4. They often wondered later what other people in the park must have thought to see them unfurl a Canadian Red Ensign, stand in line before it, throw back their shoulders, and sing "O Canada" and "The Maple Leaf Forever."

At a pause on the long climb up the great Shoshone Pass on the way to the east entrance to Yellowstone Park, the car motor refused to restart. When attempts to coax the machine to life failed, Flora set out to hitch-hike back to the town of Cody (shades of Buffalo Bill), to get help.

A friend of the operator of a service station took Flora back over the mountain road in his truck. He was the typical gangling westerner, with a "chaw of tobaccy" in one cheek, hat slouched over his eye, and a long, slow drawl. He told Flora his own favourite recreation was getting drunk — last evening, for instance. His passenger sensed that the effects hadn't yet worn off. His driving was erratic and therefore dangerous, considering the mountain roads and what one could see at some points by looking off to the side.

When spitting tobacco juice and cussing failed to help the truck driver find the trouble with the car, he enlisted the help of a tractor operator along the road, and they got the vehicle turned around in the direction from whence it had recently come. With the girls in the car, the men gave it a push and it rolled most of the way back to the town. Once in a while the tobacco-chewer would have to wham into the back bumper and give the car a shove over the next rise. He and his service-station friend finally corrected the trouble, relieved the girls of fourteen precious dollars and waved them on their way.

After three days of camping and hiking in Yellowstone Park, the girls headed north and crossed the border into Alberta, in order to be at Calgary in time for the stampede. The Lethbridge area had been lashed by a recent storm and some of the city's streets were still deep in muddy water as Dorothy manoeuvered through and pushed on to Fort MacLeod for the night.

They reached Calgary the next day, July 9, and were immediately caught up in the excitement of preparations for the stampede events two days hence. The stampede was all they had been led to believe when they were back in Montreal. They wouldn't have missed it for anything nearer than the great games festivals in Scotland.

Banff, Lake Louise, a run through the eastern portion of the great Rockies, a dip down into the United States again to see the Grand Coulee Dam, then back into Canada, through the Okanagan Valley and down the Fraser Valley, and the girls were in Vancouver on July 22, looking for temporary lodging at a YM-YWCA.

New York skyline
from Battery Point Park,
June 1955

Flora visits her
Uncle Will's family
in Pennsylvania,
June 1955 .

On the road, June 1955

Car trouble on the Buffalo Bill Highway into Yellowstone Park, July 1955

Flora and Connie leave Vancouver in April 1956.

The navigator-treasurer worked over her figures and gave a recap: fifty-three days en route; 6,409 miles; expenses for three, including capital cost for vehicle, $932.61. The breakdown for some specific items was as follows: gas and oil $122.77; lodging $188.50; food $95.29; entertainment $37.95.

With the cross-country trip behind them, the girls set out to find permanent accommodation and then work, in that order. Their common purse was almost empty. Passing through the last towns approaching Vancouver they had picked up copies of the *Vancouver Sun* and scanned the classified ads to see what accommodation was available. Now they went out to investigate various offerings. They felt it best to keep the car until they finished this running around.

After some weeding out, the girls settled for a $60-a-month apartment — the ground floor of a bungalow in a working-class district near Central Park. They didn't tell the landlady they couldn't raise $60 among them, but they made a deposit and promised to occupy a week hence. Then they headed out into the country they had just travelled through, found a berry farm whose notice for pickers they had read when they were passing through, and went to work picking raspberries.

They lived in a barn with other pickers and were in the raspberry field from 7 a.m. to 6 p.m. There had been a good deal of rain, and showers still fell at intervals. The three were soon speckled with mud and stained with berry juice. The Flora MacDonald who would one day offer herself for the political leadership of her party and country was noticed one day dunking her sandals in a horse trough, scrubbing off the mud and then putting the sandals in an oven to dry.

The picking operation netted a total of $50 and the farmer gave them twelve pounds of berries as a bonus. Back in Vancouver, they looked up a family contact, and the young wife helped them turn the berries into twenty-six bottles of jam. Rent money and food they now had. All they needed was work.

15

Sir John A —forever first

After two months in the sun the three girls from Montreal found it hard to be cooped up indoors — the two nurses at Vancouver hospitals and Flora doing stenographic work for Office Assistance Limited.

Flora was told there were roughly a hundred girls on the staff, but they saw little of one another because they were despatched here and there as extras or relief workers in a variety of offices. Only a small part of the staff remained at the central office to work on typing, bookkeeping or duplicating for customers who brought in work and called for it later in the day or week.

On Flora's second day she was assigned to a branch of the Canadian Bank of Commerce. She found that, besides differences from one bank to another, there had been many changes since she had left a Bank of Nova Scotia branch six years before.

Her work as a stenographer involved her in taking dictation and typing letters related to mortgage loans, home improvement loans and various other loans. There were plenty of forms to be filled out by applicants, as well as communications related to these forms. She had no way of knowing then that one day she would be housing critic for a political party.

For several weeks on the new job, Flora practised her shorthand and typing every night at home, to get back her old speed. If she had a Saturday off she would sometimes go to a beach, either to swim or to lie in the sun and watch liners and freighters plying their way in and out of the harbour. Her thoughts easily drifted off to her own port city of North Sydney.

The girls got rid of their car for $250. It was handier to use public transportation and save parking costs. While Flora continued to work at the same branch bank, she walked to and from work to save twenty-five cents a day.

Her most interesting assignment took her to Suite 913 of the posh Vancouver Hotel, to take some dictation from the Lord Mayor of London, England. Sir Seymour Howard dictated a speech he was to give at Calgary on the occasion of that city's fiftieth anniversary. Flora hurried off with her shorthand notes, transcribed them at the office and returned with the mayor's typed speech, ready for delivery. Sir Seymour invited her to call on him if she were ever in London.

In another of her office assignments, she worked afternoons and evenings with a Vancouver lawyer, Thomas Norris, who was conducting a major crime investigation in the city. The lawyer went on to become a Justice of the Court of Appeal of British Columbia and a significant political investigator.

A woman Flora met at church recommended her for stenographic work at British Columbia Forest Products Ltd., the biggest lumber company on the west coast. The Bank of Commerce wanted her to come on the branch's permanent staff, but a sense of loyalty to the Bank of Nova Scotia, with which she had had such a happy association in North Sydney, Peterborough and Toronto, led her to decline in favour of a position with the lumber firm.

She found herself more at ease in the relaxed atmosphere of the new office. "This is the first day in five weeks of working that has been tension free and when I haven't been expected to wear my fingers to a pulp and my nerves to a frazzle," she said. The job at Office Assistance had been good experience, but one would have needed to be constructed of iron to keep up the sustained pace.

In Vancouver she resumed her Scottish dancing lessons, and at one point, after moving from the beginning level to the intermediate level, she was talking about making a try for a teaching certificate. Her instructor had occasion, however, to reprimand her for a number of careless mistakes, and for that night at least, Flora wondered if she shouldn't think of going back to the beginners' level.

She found more time for reading than in Montreal. She let her father know she was working her way through Bruce Hutchison's *The Incredible Canadian* — a volume on Mackenzie King. "But how such a man (King) could have lasted as Canada's prime minister for such a lengthy period, fooling both friend and foe, and making a success of his career, if not always of his politics, is really incredible. The book is aptly named," she said. Later, she went on in the same vein: "The further I go into the book, the more I am amazed, astounded, revolted and fascinated by the complex actions of King, which command alternately disgust and admiration. The chapter dealing with Meighen's defeat after the 1925 schemozzle almost reduced me to tears — how King managed to pull the fat out of the fire that time is a political miracle."

Flora lined up for a university course entitled "Focus on Canada", dealing with Canada's political, economic, social and industrial problems. Following one discussion period, she said: "Last week I had to defend John A. [Macdonald] rather staunchly, as one of my classmates proceeded to erect his hero, Mackenzie King, in Macdonald's undisputed place as first statesman of the country."

Other comments she made in her weekly letters indicate that at this time she was beginning to shape her views on Canadian versus American ownership of Canadian enterprises. "It seems," she said, "that by far the greatest part of the west is United States financed and owned. Every big scheme under way here can be traced to American backing. . . . What a pity that some of the financiers of Ontario and Quebec couldn't be shaken out of their conservatism and made to realize the wonderful possibilities B.C. has to offer. I once thought that the American influence was strong in Quebec and Ontario, but it is nothing compared with the power wielded in the West. It makes one wonder about the future of these provinces as part of the Dominion of Canada."

About this time she tried to prepare her home folk for what she was sure they would think was another of her wild ideas. For some time she had kept in touch with Mrs. A. W. R. MacKenzie at the Gaelic College at St. Ann's, near her hometown. Mrs. MacKenzie had now written to ask Flora if she would consider coming to work at the college; duties would involve, besides secretarial work, meeting of visitors and some supervision of both the museum and gift shop.

Flora knew the salary would be much less than she was receiving at the lumber company office; but she was homesick. "I would love to have a summer and possibly longer in Cape Breton and especially out in the country regions," she wrote. She was now in her thirtieth year and she saw more to life than a scramble for a better and better salary.

Toward the end of the year she was summoned upstairs to the head office and told her probation period was over and the company intended to take her on permanent staff. Later she said, "I felt something of a hypocrite when the personnel manager began to talk about my two weeks' holiday next year — little does he know that I'm planning on a much longer holiday. At least I avoided joining their pension scheme for the time being."

She realized that soon she would have to let the company know of her intention to leave. Meanwhile she wrote to tell Mrs. MacKenzie at the college that she could expect her the end of the first week in June. To her folks, she said, "This West Coast is lovely, but oh, I'm so looking forward to my return to Cape Breton — that's the best thing 1956 can bring to me."

So again it was moving time for Flora MacDonald. Someone sent her a recording of Cape Breton songs, fiddle and square dance music and bagpipe solos, to add to her growing collection. "I sit and listen and laugh and cry — all at one time," she said.

That winter — her only one in Vancouver — she did some skiing on Hollyburn and Grouse Mountains. The girls had part-time use of a cabin high in the mountains. Connie and Flora started reading up on scenic areas they intended to visit in a sweep through the southern United States on their way east. Dorothy decided to remain in Vancouver. Connie intended sailing to England in July. Quite literally the old gang was breaking up, although most reluctantly.

With only ten weeks left in Vancouver, Flora commented again on her feelings about moving. "I look forward so much to new travels, but when the actual time of departure comes I'm more than a trifle sorry. When the time comes to leave Vancouver, I shall be quite regretful about leaving my job, but not the city, but I long so much to get back to Cape Breton." They planned to leave in May.

A perusal of Flora's letters at this time shows clearly that her political interests were deepening. The "Focus on Canada" lectures and discussion were striking fire in her and she was reading more in the field of policy and social problems. She was anxious to start reading the "Makers of Canada" biographical volumes.

Toward the end of March she broke the news of her leaving to her immediate superior. He was so gracious about it that Flora nearly broke down and wept. He offered her incentives to stay, but her mind was made up. "I will not be swerved," she told her family.

Two weeks before departure she outfitted herself with denim sports togs, a packsack with frame and a new camera. She planned to ship home a trunk, a set of suitcases, typewriter, books and records, and to give the rest to the local Salvation Army.

Five days ahead of leaving with Connie to hitch-hike from one coast to the other, Flora wrote her family: "Once again I shall be released from the prison walls of an office building, and breathe the clean sweet air of the open road. How content I would have been with the life of a tramp!" She indicated the route the two had planned: Victoria, Seattle, San Francisco, the Grand Canyon in Arizona, Albuquerque, Houston, New Orleans, Birmingham, Washington, New York, Boston, Montreal and North Sydney. "I guess we'll need all of six weeks to cover that little run. . . . Remember us in your prayers."

Part Four
Political Apprenticeship

16
Eureka! (I've found it!)

To ask this secretary just when it was she got into politics is almost like asking when a writer got into writing. Was it when he turned out his first book, or when he turned in his first composition in elementary school?

Flora MacDonald was brought up with wide interests — the children's classics and then the adult classics; "goings on" in her community on the island of Cape Breton, on the mainland and around the world — simply because she had a father with all-encompassing interests, who took time to pass these along to his offspring.

These interests included politics. Mr. MacDonald subscribed to five newspapers and he frequently introduced lively family discussions on political as well as other matters. Quite literally, Flora sat at her father's feet for instruction in the fundamental differences between a political Conservative and a Liberal — differences more pronounced then than now. After she went to business college, Flora found that PC workers in her community began looking to her for secretarial help at election times.

In her travels Flora had attended sessions of the British Parliament and had discussed political principles in living rooms across England and Scotland. In informal sessions in hostels all over the western continental seaboard and inland she had had long talks with student (and teacher) socialists and traded argument for argument. And she had read widely in her leisure hours when she lived in Montreal, Vancouver and Ottawa.

So it was a mature Flora MacDonald, with a broad education in political principles, who jumped into the 1956 provincial election campaign for Leonard Jones[1] in Victoria riding in Cape Breton, after she had spent a summer helping out at the Gaelic College. The girl who did nothing by halves was working so late on the first night of the campaign that Mrs. Jones had her turn in for the remainder of the night in the spare bedroom. Flora went on to occupy the room until the campaign was over. During daylight and on into the evenings, she was typing out election lists, preparing mail, contacting poll chairmen and attending workers' meetings. In spite of all this effort her candidate lost, but the Progressive Conservative Party won the province under Robert Stanfield.

It was time now for Flora to get a job that would again support her and, she hoped, give her an opportunity to travel. She went to Halifax, hoping she might get into Nova Scotia's travel bureau, but there was no opening at the time.

In May 1957, she visited her sister Sheila and some mutual friends in Toronto and her sister Jean and friends in Montreal. Then she went to Ottawa, hoping she might get into some branch of the civil service whose clerical staff might enjoy travel assignments. She considered that the Department of External Affairs would be ideal.

She stayed a few nights with Dr. and Mrs. Herbert Dorken, friends of Jean's. They helped her find an apartment in Ottawa which would accommodate her and another working girl. Flora Patterson ("Little Flora") was in Ottawa to take over a job at the new National Library, and the two Floras planned to live together. Miss MacDonald settled on an apartment near the experimental farm, for $80 a month — which was $20 a month higher than she and her two nursing friends had paid in Vancouver.

Again, with accommodation arranged, Flora set out to look for a job. Having no doubt about landing something in Ottawa, she stopped first at the main branch of the Bank of Nova Scotia and opened a small account. Then she went to the employment agency of the civil service. She filled out a job application and was told she could sit the next week for the appropriate examination.

The qualifications for a second-class stenographer were seventy words per minute for shorthand and thirty per minute for typing, so she knew she could easily qualify. Starting pay would be $220 a month.

If she could get into third-class stenography, pay would start at $250 a month, but she had been told some capable girls had found the civil service very selective when it chose senior stenos and that some girls had been in the service for years, waiting for advancement from one grade to the next. In a few days she would write that examination and then see how things turned out.

As it happened, she never wrote the exam. In the same city block as the employment agency, she came upon the headquarters of the Progressive Conservative Association of Canada and decided to go in and see if she could have her name transferred from a voting list in a Montreal riding to one in an Ottawa riding. For some reason this couldn't be done immediately, but while she was there she inquired casually if the office needed additional staff.

The receptionist said requirements had been filled. "Just for the fun of it," said Flora later, "I mentioned that I had done some work in the last provincial election in Nova Scotia." That did the trick. Flora was ushered into the office of the executive secretary, Kathleen Kearns, who told her that if she were really a good stenographer the office could use her services the next morning. She would be engaged on a weekly basis at $60 a week and would be expected to work from dawn until midnight, if the need arose. If her work wasn't up to the standard expected, she would be dismissed without any hard feelings.

A few days later, Flora wrote to her folks on the national party's office stationery: "Don't say that I didn't warn you before I left home of the type of work I would be doing when I reached Ottawa. You can see by the letterhead that I've really and truly joined the party. . . . Believe me, I'm enjoying every minute of it. My only regret is that the job is of a temporary nature, more or less from day to day, depending on the amount of work requiring attention, but I'm thrilled to have had an opportunity to play even a tiny role in the PC election machine."[2]

With the Tories cranking up for the June 10 election, Flora was sent from office to office to take on overflow work for one or another of a dozen or more stenographers. Many of these stenographers, she learned, had regular positions in the Commons as secretaries to various Conservative members. When the House had adjourned just before Easter, they had moved down to the party's headquarters, which was then at 141 Laurier Avenue West (Bracken House). Ordinarily they didn't have employment between sessions, but the party was putting in more than the usual effort to prepare for the election.

Several of the women, knowing Flora was a competent extra and was looking for permanent work, advised her to submit her name for work at the House of Commons, starting with the next session, rather than follow through with her intention of trying for the civil service elsewhere. "It certainly wouldn't do any harm to apply for a position there at the House . . . there should be a number of new men [MPs] on hand, wanting stenos, come next session," she told herself.

She was to find she wouldn't go in either direction — into the civil service in one of the scattered offices across the city or into a job as secretary to an incoming member of Parliament. She would be at the national headquarters for the next nine years — eventually as the executive secretary there, succeeding Miss Kearns. And when she would finally get to the House it would not be as a secretary but as a member of Parliament, looking for one or more secretaries to work for her.

In the role of an extra at headquarters Flora found the first weeks varied and exciting. She took long units of dictation from the men in charge of party leader John Diefenbaker's speaking itinerary and the itineraries of other prominent party men, like Donald Fleming and Léon Balcer[3]. Then she transcribed the speeches into typescript, ready for delivery. She took dictation, as well, for speeches to be given on television and radio broadcasts on a national scale. She had a feeling of being "in" on matters of national importance.

When she wasn't doing these chores, she was cutting stencils listing the various candidates, with brief biographies of each. Or she was filling orders for pamphlets and other propaganda items originating at headquarters.

She tells her father that if he is on the receiving end of a pamphlet describing John Diefenbaker's new national policy, or some other pamphlet obviously from headquarters, his daughter may have had a hand in its preparation. She tells him that she and some of the other girls worked overtime for a couple of evenings, typing eighteen thousand envelopes addressed to all the voters in Mr. Diefenbaker's own personal riding. "I don't know how much longer this job can continue for me, but I'm supposed to remain until this Saturday."

A week later she was still there and had been told she would be needed until at least the June 10 election. What would happen then she wasn't sure. To be on the safe side, she at last filed an application with the civil service.

Enthusiasm was mounting day by day. One night she attended a rally of the opposing Liberals at the local Coliseum. She came away with the impression that Liberal Prime Minister St. Laurent "acted like a tired old man." The impression added new hopes that Mr. Diefenbaker could defeat him.

The final stages of the campaign seemed to have degenerated into trivialities and mud-slinging — sure sign, she said, of the absence of any really vital issues. The major issue should have been the supremacy of Parliament in the wake of the pipeline debate. Nevertheless, "we've had great reports of the enthusiastic gatherings which are featuring Mr. Diefenbaker's progress through the west," she told her home folks.

A week before the election she wrote home again, observing that she had now passed her thirty-first birthday and could no longer be identified with the youthful twenties. Around the headquarters office she said there was the realization that in just one more week the "shouting, the hullaballoo and the pressurized preparation of the last few months will have run their course — and a good many people will be relaxing for the first time in weeks, that is, if they are still conscious."

The spirit of optimism was increasing daily. "Reports of the reception being accorded Mr. Diefenbaker, wherever he stops, continue to build up our hopes, and though we may be whistling in the dark, there is a definite feeling in the air that a certain amount of change [of seats] will take place. Work has kept us in a constant pitch here at the office, and there's no talk of my leaving until after the election — and perhaps not even then," she wrote.

She was still doing radio and television scripts and thought that Mr. Diefenbaker's last one was "especially well written and of a high moral character." She noted that he had a team of writers working for him all the time but that Mr. Diefenbaker didn't rely word for word on their scripts. Nor did he use notes. "He must have a phenomenal memory," she observed.

Late on election day, as the results from the east were the first to be relayed by teletype to the national office, Flora was given the job of sending these by open-line telephone to the Chief's campaign office in Prince Albert. At first she could hardly credit what she was reading on the machine's printout. As one Liberal seat after another fell, she was almost beside herself with joy.

Mr. Diefenbaker had voted in Prince Albert and later in the evening had gone to Regina to appear on the national television network. He heard the last of the ballot results on the plane.[4] The final tabulation showed 113 PC seats to the Liberals' 106 — a Conservative victory for the first time since 1930 under R. B. Bennett. But the victors would constitute a minority government, subject to defeat on every vote in the next Parliament. The CCF had obtained 25 seats, the Social Credit 19 and Independents 2.

Mr. Diefenbaker was welcomed in Ottawa three days later by jubilant, placard-waving Tories, including Flora MacDonald. A few days later, the Liberals turned over to the Conservatives the stewardship they had enjoyed for decades, and on June 21 — eleven days after his electoral triumph — Mr. Diefenbaker was officially sworn in as the head of the new government, the thirteenth Prime Minister of Canada.

At the party's national office the mix of workers was rescrambled. Once cabinet ministers were appointed, their secretaries, many of whom had been at headquarters, were recalled. That left only Flora and two others to carry on, under the office manager, in place of the former staff of fourteen. Then one of the other two left to join her husband and family in a move out of the city. Flora's only secretary associate became private secretary to Davie Fulton in the House. On July 2, Flora became assistant secretary to the national director, Allister Grosart, who had been campaign manager and was now the Prime Minister's chief adviser.

In four weeks Flora had gone from being an extra pair of hands in preparation for an election to secretary for the Prime Minister's chief adviser. She may well have pondered the little ditty she had learned in her youth:

> Down to perdition and up to the throne,
> He travels fastest who travels alone.

---

[1] Not to be confused with another Leonard Jones, who became mayor of Moncton, an Independent MP and a controversial figure in the 1976 leadership race.

[2] I am following Miss MacDonald's own written account of how she came to work at the national headquarters, rather than an often-repeated version which differs slightly.

[3] Mr. Diefenbaker had been party leader since December 1956, having made it to that position on his third try, at age 61. The earlier attempts had been in 1942 and 1948.

[4] Patrick Nicholson, *Vision and Indecision*, p. 52.

17

The Tory encyclopedia

In nine years at the national headquarters of the Progressive Conservative Party, Flora MacDonald gained insights and managerial skills that experienced politicians might well have envied. As Mr. Grosart's personal and confidential secretary she was right at the heart of the party's operations. She was detached enough to judge just how effective were the persons, policies and methods involved. After her first few weeks at the national headquarters, Flora MacDonald was never again just a stenographer, but a working partner; and later she was executive secretary, with all that this implied.

Her keen interest in all kinds of people — what would eventually be called her populist appeal — had been evident for many years before she got into politics. Now, through the normal relations Tory members had with their party headquarters and through a certain amount of socializing, she got to know most of the Conservative MPs on a first-name basis, and in some instances, their wives and friends as well.

The same went for the civil service, and particularly for parliamentary assistants and their staffs. She saw the whole Tory fraternity, not only for what its members were around the Commons, but in their after hours too. The same was true, although to a lesser degree, for her acquaintance with some Liberals and members of the minority parties.

Her knowledge of her own party was extended, bit by bit, to practically every riding across Canada. And as she got to know riding personnel, she was the one that constituency people were apt to ask for first when they came to Ottawa, or the one they asked for when they placed a telephone call. She was easy to talk to.

This acquaintance with ridings led her to perceive sectional and regional differences. Canada, she soon found, was not a unified mass of people with a single outlook and similar problems. There were many little Canadas — regions with their own long traditions and felt needs. Flora got to know how people in each region tended to feel about their existence and what they considered Ottawa should do for them.

Along with her knowledge of people, she got to know policies as well, as she took down statements in shorthand and transcribed them for speeches and pamphlets and as she helped to flesh out statements. When a blue pencil was drawn through some wording and a refinement indicated, she grasped the implications of the change. Many times she chuckled, and at others winced, when she knew that statements were being left deliberately ambiguous for subtle reasons.

She was equally well acquainted with policy statements made in caucus, in committees and in the House. It is not saying too much to affirm that in her later years at headquarters, Flora MacDonald was probably one of the best informed Conservatives in Ottawa and recognized as such.

As she got to know people and policies, she got to know promotional methods. She learned the best approach to get action in a given riding in Newfoundland, Winnipeg or Victoria: a telephone call, a letter, a telegram or a personal visit.

She learned to appreciate that there were many ways of gearing up for an election. Her memory became a ways and means bag, into which she could dip when riding association people contacted the central office and said: "We've tried everything and nothing seems to work." She learned what resources the party could count on — where to go for expert research; how the news media operate and what aspects of a campaign are apt to be considered newsworthy; how some advertising firms are better than others.

And then there was her own experience in successive campaigns. No wonder that, with a tough election or by-election coming up, the cry would sometimes go out, "Send us Flora!" She was dashing from one campaign to another and having virtual management of some of them — and loving every minute of it.

A perusal of Miss MacDonald's correspondence during those nine years indicates how thoroughly she took to politics. The fact that she remained in the national office for nine years, which was longer than she had remained anywhere, indicates that at last she had found something that satisfied an inner quest.

Heretofore, routine office work had challenged her at first because it dealt with a new area of interest and gave her a chance to prove she could be both efficient and fast. When the job became boring she had to move on. But politics, a pursuit as broad as life itself, and touching people in their daily lives, was different. It allowed for the stimulating exchange of ideas and for travel. It was an adventure, because it was a battle of wits, whose outcome was always shrouded for a while in uncertainty, as surely as Cape Breton hills are often shrouded in mist. Here Flora was to feel at home.

She would leave politics only if she were thrust out — as happened. And then she would come round to it another way. Kicked out the door, she would return by the window.

Some of her experiences during her first years at the national headquarters left lasting impressions. The thrill of helping Prime Minister Diefenbaker come to power carried over to those few times when he dropped in at party headquarters. Flora MacDonald was not a little girl in ringlets and all agog because a great man crossed the threshold where she worked. She was a mature young woman who had already met Canadian and British statesmen. Her home training and Calvinistic background had made respect for her elders and for rulers a matter of feeling as well as of principle. If the Chief had glowered at her she would have accepted it, but when his blue eyes lit up with laughter and the two swapped stories about her namesake of sorts, the great John A. Macdonald, Flora was elated.

When her work was over for the day, if the House was in session and she had learned that the Prime Minister was going to speak on some issue, she would often slip into a gallery to listen. She and other staff members would unfailingly listen to broadcast speeches.

Writing home, Flora said: "I don't know if any of you heard Mr. Diefenbaker's speech a week ago Saturday in Dartmouth, when he spoke so frankly and forthrightly about U.S.-Canadian economic relations, but I think it was one of the best jobs he ever did." Again, she wrote: "Yesterday I slipped away from the office early to hear Mr. Diefenbaker's reply to Mr. Pearson's criticisms, and the PM was in good form."

A layoff of miners in Cape Breton naturally aroused Flora's interest. Debate on possible federal help carried over into an evening session in the Commons. Flora wrote home in glowing terms about the Prime Minister's speech. "Nothing I've ever heard there came anywhere near equalling the PM. . . . As Charles Lynch (who is anything but friendly to us) put it: 'Having dispensed with these formalities, the Prime Minister drew himself up to his full stature and delivered the finest speech of his career.' "

Even before Flora was placed in charge of office routine and staff, she was asked by Mr. Grosart to take complete charge of an anniversary dinner for Mr. Diefenbaker at the Chateau Laurier Hotel. It meant handling all arrangements, invitations, menus and even the presentations.

An illuminated address was prepared for the occasion, and the Chief was presented with a thirteen-volume set of the Oxford Dictionary. The guest list had been expanded several times until it included about three hundred men, including MPs, senators and other special friends. Mrs. Diefenbaker and five other women were the only non-males invited to share the great dining room. Flora was given the honour of escorting the Diefenbakers to their places at the head table. She was also the one who later gathered up all the presentation gifts and took them around to the Prime Minister's residence.

During this time, Flora took driving lessons and bought herself a car. She tore around the country every weekend she wasn't working; she visited family and friends and took in a variety of cultural events.

She treated herself to an extended vacation trip to Britain and the Continent in 1963. This time, she flew to London, where she attended sessions of the House of Commons before renting a car and driving north. After calling on relatives at Altrincham, she revisited old friends all over Scotland. Again she stayed in hostels, but having a car, she loaded it up each morning with hitch-hikers and took them with her — her way of paying back the debt she felt she owed to drivers back in 1952 and 1953.

She visited France, Italy and Greece, Austria, Switzerland and the little principality of Liechtenstein in the Alps. From there she sent a card to Mr. Diefenbaker, whose consent had been given for her longer-than-usual vacation.

18
Another bump...another boost

To say that Flora MacDonald's nine years at headquarters were valuable years for her later political career is not to overlook the fact that they contained sadness too — and one *particularly* sad event.

There were events and trends in those years, particularly in the last few, that gave many Conservatives misgivings about the party leadership, which had been in Mr. Diefenbaker's hands since 1956. They saw the party peak, electorally, in the 1958 election, capturing 208 votes to the Liberals' 49; but then four years later it lost 92 seats, while the liberals gained 51.

Flora retained her confidence in the Prime Minister long after some of those closest to him in the Administration had apparently lost it. Mr. Diefenbaker had always been something of a hero to her — a Sir Lancelot galloping off to do battle with giants. She would always respect him and insist that others respect him. She treasured a photograph of the two of them that he had given her, with a warm inscription across the face of it praising Flora for her contributions to the Conservative Party.

The leader's old charisma was still there. His public performances were still good. Give him a theme and an audience and he was a force to be reckoned with. The orator with the golden voice could lash a crowd until it bowed its collective head with feelings of shame, or he could bring it to its feet with wild cheering.

This was the public Diefenbaker. But where Flora worked, behind the scenes, she could see that the party was worried about its leader's indecisiveness after his relatively narrow 1962 victory. By late 1962, a gradual rift had formed between the Prime Minister and at least ten of his Cabinet ministers. Lacking confidence in his ministers, Diefenbaker consulted them less and less[1] and made some policy decisions completely on his own. The government, as such, had ceased to govern, and Canada's image abroad had deteriorated. Before tendering his resignation, Minister of National Defence Douglas Harkness denounced Mr. Diefenbaker before the cabinet and said the entire country had lost its respect for him and confidence in his leadership.

Following Mr. Diefenbaker's 1963 defeat as Prime Minister, fifteen Conservative MPs "were daring enough to urge policy reform and a leadership review."[2] Before the year was out, some constituency organizations had passed motions favouring a leadership convention. Later, Léon Balcer, member for Three Rivers, led Quebec Tories in calling for a leadership convention, but the attempt to oust Diefenbaker was frustrated at the level of the Conservative executive.

Like a number of other party supporters, Flora had tried to persuade herself that things weren't as bad as they seemed. True, there were dark days prior to the 1963 election, when she wanted to quit before the inevitable happened — before the aging leader, who apparently couldn't see his shortcomings, would bring the party down with him in the coming election. But she hung on through the election, hoping for the best.

Then came the 1965 election and Mr. Diefenbaker's second failure to form a government. In that crisis Flora shared his anguish. Her feelings for the man and her fierce loyalty to the party made her ashamed of a half-formed resolve to quit. This was her party, "for richer, for poorer, in sickness and in health" — hadn't she heard that at a dozen weddings and translated it into a different context? She must see things through.

Added to her feelings of loyalty to the party were reservations relating to her family. Particularly in the eyes of her father, who had stuck to one job all his life, this daughter of his had quit too many jobs. At times he must see his Flora as inconstant, a gypsy, a bee flitting from one flower to another. She simply could not write home and say, "Well, folks, I've done it again." Her anxiety sat grinning at her as she worked.

She knew that, sooner or later, she would have to choose between standing with or against The Chief, as she became more and more convinced he was becoming a party liability. How easily it would resolve itself if Mr. Diefenbaker would only decide on his own to resign as party leader, while remaining as a member of Parliament! Others in the party were saying the same, but Mr. Diefenbaker, while threatening to resign, couldn't bring himself to it.

If Flora had been a mere secretary in the office, fulfilling orders, she might have been able to keep her feelings to herself and carry on. But for some time she had been a consultant and participant. To back off now and try to take a neutral position would be phony as well as cowardly. She agreed that there should be a leadership convention, and if Mr. Diefenbaker decided to stand, this was a democratic right she would defend. But she could no longer conscientiously support his candidacy. She was known to be weighing, with other Conservatives, alternative possibilities.

When Flora MacDonald is asked what was the worst thing that ever happened to her, and then the best, she can give a single answer: being fired. That 1966 experience seemed at first a malicious act. To be thrust out of the party's national office when it was there that she had worked harder than she had ever worked in her life — which is saying a lot, considering how Flora put herself into every job — seemed not only inconsiderate but cruel. She was fired under suspicion of disloyalty when she felt she was being supremely loyal to high principle.

It wasn't that her dismissal was althogether a surprise. She telephoned a Queen's University professor several nights before the axe fell and said, "I think I'm going to be fired." She knew that in voicing her own misgivings to key party persons who had broken with Mr. Diefenbaker she was placing herself on a collision course. She knew enough about goings on behind the scenes to perceive that the axe blade was being honed.

Who did the firing is a matter of record. It was James Johnston, the party's national director in 1966, who felt that too much power was in Flora MacDonald's hands. Coming as he did, in some senses, as an outsider (a businessman and not a politician) to his prestigious post, he may understandably have been irritated by Flora's superior knowledge, influence and even manner. Rightly or wrongly he may have taken the executive secretary's explanations and objections as challenges to his competence. The male ego finds it hard to be corrected and guided by a woman whose position ranks her as inferior.

In his book, entitled *The Party's Over*, Dr. Johnston relates some of the changes he effected at headquarters, including eliminating the telephone switchboard to save $600 a month. "I also asked Flora MacDonald to resign, and moved Marcel Bureau into her office next my own," he wrote.[3] "I deliberately let the rest of the staff disappear before walking down to Miss MacDonald's office to tell her. I said she should take as many months as she wanted to find another position and could keep on with her job in the meantime or take a holiday. I also told her that three months' severance pay would be coming to her."[4]

When Dr. Johnston told Mr. Diefenbaker the next morning, the party leader said, "Good — I was wondering when it was ever going to happen," according to Johnston's version of the incident.[5]

Robert Chambers, political cartoonist for the Halifax *Chronicle-Herald* dashed off a cartoon, which he labelled "Great Moments in History: Bonnie Prince Charlie Bids Farewell to Flora MacDonald." The cartoon shows Mr. Diefenbaker as "MacDief the Rightful King," in a kilt, standing on the rocky shore of the Isle of Skye, but with the House of Commons in the background. MacDief is casting adrift a frail female in an equally frail rowboat. The matching caption says: "The Conservative Party fires its most dedicated worker."

The literature gathering around Flora MacDonald's dismissal makes several things clear. The view that a leadership review was necessary and that at a duly called leadership convention Mr. Diefenbaker must be replaced, whether he liked it or not, by somebody more likely to win the 1968 election and heal the party of its divisions wasn't Flora's view alone. She wasn't a lone rebel. She wasn't even one of a pair of rebels — the other one reputedly being Dalton Camp. Flora's open identification with the "dump Dief" forces came *after* her firing, not before. Long before that, as has been indicated, there had been a growing disaffection within the party over Mr. Diefenbaker's leadership.

Flora was only one dissatisfied Tory, but she was one at headquarters, and that made a difference. She was not an innocent little girl sucked into a conspiracy and brainwashed by Dalton Camp, as is sometimes hinted. She was as knowledgeable as anyone on how the party had gone downhill and was likely to suffer in the next election. If her experience was used by Camp, it was after her firing, as a symbol of how far suspicion and unreason could go.

The issue here has sometimes been given an immoral cast, as if sympathy on Flora's part for a leadership review, and activity in keeping with that sympathy, while she was still an employee, was unethical. This sounds reasonable, but taken as a principle, it would mean that reform of organizations should never be initiated from within. On that view, the church, the labour movement and all other movements should never be reformed by those inside, who are in a position to see the faults. They could only be reformed by those already outside or those who would jump outside. And then the question would arise: when should would-be reformers take their leave from inside, lest they be branded as traitors?

The chances are high that, for all her anguish at the direction events had been taking, Flora would never have voluntarily quit her job. She would have stayed in the headquarters nest for some years more if somebody hadn't taken a stick and turned her out. Miss Indispensable had to be thrown out on her ear in order to pick herself up and make full use of her potential.

Any perceptive person around Ottawa could have said what Professor John Meisel of Queen's University has said of those years in the national office: "She was an under-recognized person." She was sitting on a stump, whittling, when she had it in her to be building bridges.

Being fired was, on this broader view, a good thing. She couldn't see this at the time. She felt like a wounded animal. She wanted to crawl away and lick her wounds. She felt rejected and alone — more alone than she had ever felt in her life. She nursed a sorrow that, for the moment, no one could share, even though she had dozens of close friends. Her Calvinistic background ("Touch not the Lord's anointed") had given her some sleepless nights until she had satisfied herself that she could stand with Luther and say, "I could do nothing else, so help me, God!"

It was obvious that Flora MacDonald was making a painful choice between loyalty to a person and loyalty to party and principle. She chose the latter, and as events were to prove, found herself propelled on a course that led to a political career of her own.

As Professor Hugh Thorburn of Queen's political studies department states: "Flora's dismissal threw her out of the party organization and therefore made her a free-wheeling individual who wasn't an employee any more. But she was still a Tory and very highly regarded. This incident called forth a great deal of sympathy for her. If she had continued as a party bureaucrat she would simply have been a knowledgeable person behind the scenes, without great personal significance. Her dismissal turned into a public figure a person who would not otherwise have been one. The incident made her available for high office."[6]

In line with the professor's remarks that Flora was still a loyal Tory was the fact that following her dismissal and after she left headquarters, she went to Prince Edward Island to help the Conservative premier, Walter Shaw, with his campaign.

When the leadership convention was held in 1967, Flora worked strenuously for the election of Robert Stanfield, which was very understandable. She had helped get him elected as premier of Nova Scotia in 1956 and re-elected in 1960 and later elections.

Meanwhile, Queen's University's political studies department, knowing Flora was available for employment, snapped at the chance of getting her to join the department.

---

[1] Once he called them a "nest of traitors," (Peter Newman, *Renegade in Power*, p. 363).

[2] Peter Newman, *The Distemper of Our Times*, p. 96.

[3] James Johnston, *The Party's Over*, p. 82.

[4] *Loc. cit.*

[5] It wasn't long after this, when Mr. Stanfield came to power as party leader, that Dr. Johnston was summoned to the Stanfield office. The message was delivered by Mr. Stanfield's press secretary, who happened to be Flora MacDonald's brother Ronald. "Do you know what he wants?" asked Johnston. "I think he's going to fire you, Jim," was MacDonald's reply. (From an interview.)

[6] An interview.

19
Among the eggheads

Miss MacDonald's acceptance of a job at Queen's University wasn't a case of "any old port in a storm." The experience of life in a university community was one she had missed in her youth. She was glad to get around to it at last, although she was not going as a student.

By now, in many ways, she had more than compensated for the lack of a university training. She had read and travelled widely and had attended more cultural performances than many an English or history professor ever sees. She had discussed life in general, as well as politics in particular, with academics and non-academics as she made her way across several countries. She had audited university courses on the side. And in nine years — which is more than twice the span of most university programs — she had worked side by side, in Ottawa, with graduate researchers and a professional elite.

But a campus experience she had missed. "Some day . . . some day," she had said. That "some day" had come.

Professor John Meisel, then head of Queen's political studies department, had met Flora several years before when he was doing research for a book on the 1957 election. At the PC national office Flora had been "tremendously helpful" (his own words). In the professor's travels across Canada, gathering facts and impressions, he had run into Flora in her other capacity as a much-sought-after campaign worker. She had left a deep impression of her political know-how — and her know-who.

Once, in Ottawa, he had told her that if she ever wanted a job she was to let him know. "I'm sure somebody like you could be used at

Queen's," he said. They had laughed about it because Flora wasn't interested at that time. So, when Flora phoned the professor from Winnipeg and said, "I think I'm going to be fired — what about that job?" he said to himself, "Gee, Flora would be marvellous" (again, his own words). By June he had cleared the way for her to come to Queen's as an executive officer in the political studies department. Her duties were to be mainly administrative.

The timing for Flora was perfect. She was dismissed in April. Taking national party director James Johnston at his word, she took the option of leaving immediately with three months severance pay. The interval before the opening of a new session at Queen's gave her a chance to help Walter Shaw. She was still a loyal Tory, with the sympathy and respect of most Tories, although she had fallen out with the ruling powers at headquarters. The interval also gave her a chance to visit her family and return to some of her beloved nature spots in Cape Breton.

By mid-August she had settled in an upstairs apartment in Kingston and had begun her work. In an expanding department, with a staff of sixteen or seventeen, her duties were varied. She had to integrate the professors' teaching and tutorial schedules and match classrooms with timetables. She had to order textbooks, supplies and equipment, approve department bills and draw up next year's budget.

Each session had its visiting professors, whose flight schedules, accommodation and expenses had to be looked after. Correspondence with prospective political science students, and especially with students working at the graduate level, involved letters of reference, transcripts of credit and discussion of programs.

As students gradually became aware of how politically knowledgeable Flora was, they would consult her about regional characteristics and differences, federal and provincial policy, legislation, regulations, procedures, personnel, and even about prevailing moods in the House and in the electorate. Some of these one-to-one consultations flowed over into after-hours discussion groups, as Flora indicated her readiness to talk politics at any time, anywhere. Many of these students are now in civil service or political posts across the country.

The administrator-consultant's aptitude and willingness led quite naturally, as time moved along, to some tutorial work for the department. Students in a course on Canadian government met with Miss MacDonald once a week for discussion of textbook and supplementary reading material, classroom lectures and whatever other relevant

Flora at work . . .

. . . and at play

ideas came to bear on the subject. "Her firsthand knowledge always led to lively discussions," said Professor Hugh Thorburn, who became department head in 1968, succeeding Professor Meisel. "She had a lot to tell that wasn't in textbooks."

For some of her routine work, stenographers and typists were available, but Flora, a work addict herself and better at some of the routine jobs than run-of-the-mill office workers, would often do the work herself. Even after several years at the university, she found it difficult to delegate. Rather than assign work to someone else she might stay after hours and do it herself. Then, when her nerves were a-jangle from overstress and she saw other staff members off playing, she might begin to pity herself. It was a common enough human failing, and eventually she learned the art of delegating work.

As if she weren't doing enough already, Flora occasionally wrote academic papers for delivery at political workshops, on or off campus. One of these, on the theme of electoral and party reform, was given at the Niagara Falls 1969 conference on Progressive Conservative priorities for Canada. The paper called on party policy makers to face up to the need for grassroots discussion on all aspects of social and economic life.

Flora reminded her audience that other organizations, like the Canadian Manufacturers' Association, the Canadian Chamber of Commerce and the Boy Scouts Association, by definition, have narrow interests, but a political party must be concerned about the whole of people's lives. This means more than springing into life only when an election approaches. Between elections the party associations should help to "ensure the continued well-being of our democratic system," by helping to formulate party policy.

Flora told the delegates that if she had her way there would be policy conferences at three levels — constituency, regional and national. "We can't let the burden of policy-making fall solely on our MPs." Policy statements, ground out at whatever level, have an educative value, she said, not only for the participants and for the party that receives the statements, but for the general public — the electorate.

She faulted her party leaders in general terms — no names mentioned — for not encouraging an upward communication flow. All the communication, as she well knew, was downward, from the party bigwigs to the constituencies. "Dissent, rather than being encouraged as a means of focusing awareness, is equated with disloyalty." (How well she knew that from experience!) Being charged with creating tension within the party structure didn't bother her as much as the

100

possibility that at the grassroots level lack of action would make a political party "increasingly irrelevant."

She told the delegates too that at the constituency level there is a job to do in helping to create a public conscience on social issues like poverty, drugs, law reform, housing, penal reform and status of minority groups. Political parties simply can't leave it to pressure groups, protest movements, student activists and social planning councils to be the agents of change — not if political parties want to be considered relevant when they present candidates at the next election.

Such statements, coming out of her years at Queen's, indicated that while she was still as much a Tory as ever, she was an advocate of reform. She was what the full party name declared — a *Progressive* Conservative.

20
Stanfield wins the ticket

Flora MacDonald's heavy involvement in political studies at the university and her occasional participation in off-campus political functions by no means took up all her time or energy. By the time the PC Association held its annual meeting in November 1966, the wound to MacDonald pride had healed and she was ready to plunge into party politics again.

Her dismissal had been the act of a minority — although a high-placed minority: the Leader of Her Majesty's Loyal Opposition and his director of the headquarters staff. Many Conservatives — MPs, senators and other party members — deplored the act.

Despite her recent rebuff, Flora campaigned for the post of national secretary, and won it; it was the first time the position had been won by a woman. Dalton Camp was elected as national president by a smaller majority. This development was not likely to please Mr. Diefenbaker, but the mood of the annual meeting didn't run in that direction anyway.

Flora's honour that day was not her old paid position at headquarters restored. But the new position, which she could easily carry along with her position at Queen's, had a measure of prestige and political clout far beyond that of a manager of the national office.

The annual meeting had set a date in 1967 for a leadership convention. Conservatives identifying with Dalton Camp's position on leadership review were anxious to see candidates offer themselves who would have some hope of rescuing party leadership from Mr. Diefenbaker.

Few Conservatives had any doubts about Dalton Camp's wanting the position himself, although he was cagey about saying so. "Lest you show conflict of interest, you'd better resign as president before announcing," was Flora's advice. She showed herself willing to support Camp's candidacy until it became clear that Robert Stanfield was offering himself. Then both Camp and Flora gave their support to the then Nova Scotia premier. To Camp's credit he wrote the first draft of Mr. Stanfield's announcement.

Eventually there were eleven leadership candidates in the field: John Diefenbaker, Donald Fleming, Davie Fulton, Alvin Hamilton, George Hees, John Maclean, Wallace McCutcheon, Duff Roblin, Mary Sawka, Michael Starr and Robert Stanfield. With Flora working in the front lines, the Stanfield forces took the none-too-sparkling Nova Scotian before 2,256 delegates in Toronto's Maple Leaf Gardens and brought him off a winner.

Political journalist Geoffrey Stevens described the scene and pointed out its significance for future leadership conventions:

The Conservative leadership convention was an extravaganza that deserved all the superlatives heaped on it. For the first time, a Canadian political party had set out to emulate in scale and style an American presidential nominating convention. It had marching bands and balloons and pretty girls by the hundreds, floor demonstrations, and lavish cocktail parties for thousands. It was a great show and it made great television. More than that, it had great drama. Would John Diefenbaker attempt one last stand? Or would he accept the inevitable and quietly receive the honours due to him, allowing the party to choose his successor? Could the Conservatives find any man with the patience, understanding, and tact needed to reverse the centrifugal forces that seemed determined to tear the party to pieces? Partly because it was the first convention of its kind and partly because of the Diefenbaker drama, the Conservative convention occupies a special place in the memories of the people who were there. It had an excitement that not even the Liberals could match seven months later when they met to elect Pierre Elliott Trudeau, the most intriguing political figure of the age. The Tory convention is the yardstick by which all other leadership conventions must be measured.[1]

In the 1967 convention, Mr. Diefenbaker received only 271 votes to Mr. Stanfield's 519 on the first ballot. The old chieftain's count fell to

172 on the second ballot, to Stanfield's 613. Diefenbaker dropped out after the third ballot. Roblin was the toughest contender after that, but he succumbed to Stanfield on the fifth and final ballot.

Flora MacDonald and a fellow Cape Bretoner embraced in the centre of the hall.[2] What a story it all made when Flora repeated it to staff and students back at Queen's University.

[1] Geoffrey Stevens, *Stanfield*, p. 188, reprinted by permission of the Canadian publishers, McClelland and Stewart, Toronto.
[2] *Ibid.*, p. 195.

21
Who'll be house mother?

It has been said that if you want something done it's best to go to a busy person rather than to one who is idle. The busy person is already in motion. Back in 1968 the Kingston Elizabeth Fry Society followed this principle and recruited Flora MacDonald as president.

The society was involved at the time in an important venture: the launching of Canada's first halfway house for women inmates in the federal prison system. Workers recognized that the jump from prison life to a free society was so big that some girls and women couldn't make it. Hence the halfway house concept.

The idea was to provide a home in the community where selected female inmates could live during the final months of their sentence, instead of at the Kingston Prison for Women. They could go out to work or to school during the daytime and return to the house by the curfew hour. The home setting would enable the occupants to take some responsibility for themselves and participate in community activities along with school or employment.

The idea had been proposed by the federal Department of the Solicitor-General at least four years earlier, but implementation had been frustrated by one thing after another. Officials first said they couldn't find qualified personnel to run such a house. Then they came up with the idea of having a superintendent, five guidance officers, a stenographer and two housekeepers — all for a household limiting the inmate intake to about six persons.

The Elizabeth Fry Society strongly favoured the basic idea of a halfway house, while doubting the need for such a large paid staff.

The society had been working in the Prison for Women since the late 1940s and had been involved in a pre-release program since 1956. The program then had been simply a matter of arranging for the female inmate to live with a family in the community for the last two weeks of her sentence, as an aid to adjusting again to life outside prison walls.

But when officials in the prison system proposed using a former warden's house on the Collins Bay Penitentiary premises, with a chauffeur service to Kingston, members of the society protested that this would defeat the self-help purpose of the program. They wanted a house, or even an apartment, away from the prison atmosphere and nearer to the central area, where the girls and women would be likely to find work and cultural activities.

At this time the society was looking for a president to succeed Mrs. Rene Hogarth. What was needed was a dynamic leader to bring to fruition the now somewhat confused plans for a halfway house and to continue and expand Elizabeth Fry prison programs. Flora's well-known organizational ability, knowledge of the intricate workings of government departments and concern for social problems led the Elizabeth Fry executive to ask Flora, who was then in her second year of administration at Queen's, to consider taking on yet another responsibility.

Miss Kathleen Healey of Queen's Extension Department, who was a founding member and past president of the society, and retiring president Rene Hogarth took Flora to lunch at the university Faculty Club and asked her to take on the job.

Flora had a busy on-campus program — administration, counselling and some teaching — and off-campus she was involved in the work of the National Progressive Conservative Association, with an occasional election campaign somewhere across the country thrown in. But participation in the community was something she had talked about at length in the political context. Here was an opportunity to practise what she preached. The disadvantaged always had a large place in her thoughts. She took on the job with characteristic zeal and served for two years as president.

The society credits her with cutting through red tape, flattening objections, and finally getting the halfway house underway. The Solicitor-General's department, half committed to the idea and half-persuaded it wouldn't work, was glad to see local initiative. The society went looking for a house away from any of the prisons, and the department agreed to move the furnishings from the former

106

warden's house. The society raised $7,000 toward the first year's operation, and a matching grant was obtained from the federal government.

Flora and her associates found a five-bedroom house in a suitable residential area, and Flora and the past president talked to people in the neighbourhood, to allay their worst fears. They received enough co-operation, along with the blessing of the city fathers, to make it safe to proceed. A house mother was established in the rented Elizabeth Fry house, and the place was open for business.

Arrangements for inmates ready for parole were relatively simple. Applications, voluntarily made, had to be approved by both the society and the prison, and any of the parties to the arrangement could cancel at any time.

House rules were kept to a minimum, and volunteers from the society took over occasionally for the house mother when she wanted to be free for an evening. They also did voluntary housework. The halfway house was considered such a success that units of the Elizabeth Fry Society proceeded to open similar houses in many cities, especially in the western provinces.

The opening of the house in Kingston, in April 1970, was not Flora's only major involvement with the society. Along with other society members she took part in a visitation program within the prison walls. Visitors made themselves available for conversation; they conducted sewing classes and classes in various crafts, depending on the interests of the inmates; they held bingos and even some dances. For the latter, they brought in male law students from Queen's. From her wide contacts, Flora was able to arrange for many outside groups of entertainers to visit the women's prison.

When the "occasional pass" system came into vogue, female inmates were allowed to visit in the homes of Elizabeth Fry members or to be taken to community events and then returned to custody. Flora often had the girls and women to her apartment for an evening with her folk records, tales of her adventures across Canada or overseas, or just a chat about problems in our kind of society. Such an evening would be topped off with a snack.

On other occasions, Flora would turn up at a community concert or play with a friend in tow. She always introduced her as a friend and never as an inmate. Rene Hogarth said Flora had the happy faculty of being able to relate to people as people, regardless of their station in life or their present circumstances.

While she was at Queen's and involved in the Elizabeth Fry Society, it was pressed on Flora, late in 1969, that she had considerable vacation time owing to her. "I bundled it all together," she said, "along with a return ticket and a few essentials and took off for India for a couple of months. Hitch-hiking in India is tough. Travelling third class isn't much better, but it can be done, and you get to know a great deal about the country as you go.

"I had attended many political meetings in my life prior to that time, but never one to compare to an open-air annual convention of the Congress Party when Prime Minister Indira Gandhi addressed an assembled audience of over 400,000 people. The meaning of the words 'population explosion' becomes very real to you, and with a sense of panic and claustrophobia, when you find yourself caught up in a crowd of that magnitude.

"No one who has ever been to India will again be free of what it means to see starvation and distress unknown to our western democracies — a distress which it is impossible to convey, even given the wonders of television. It was a searing experience, a gripping experience, but one which has made me appreciate the necessity for the redistribution of the world's resources."

Back in Kingston in January, Flora went on with her work at Queen's and with the Elizabeth Fry Society. As things were to work out, she would retain her interest in the Elizabeth Fry chapter, even after moving to Ottawa as a member of Parliament. When families of inmates would contact her, either in Ottawa or at her constituency office in Kingston, asking her to do something, she often contacted the society to see what support it could render. She kept the chapter aware of current or pending legislation touching inmates and their care. And, of course, she did the same for the John Howard Society, whose main concern was for male inmates.

22
On the stump

Flora MacDonald was recruited for still another side job soon after the founding, in Toronto, of the non-partisan Committee for an Independent Canada, in 1970. The committee arose out of a luncheon meeting at which Walter Gordon, former Liberal finance minister, Peter Newman, editor of *Maclean's* magazine, and Abraham Rotstein, Toronto economist, shared their concern over the extent to which the Canadian economy was being taken over by the United States.

Mr. Gordon had already published two books airing the subject. The first, entitled *Troubled Canada*, outlined the need for new domestic policies. The second, entitled *A Choice for Canada*, warned that Canada was almost imperceptibly slipping back into colonial status.

The luncheon group was not anti-American in sentiment. Its members were simply hard-headed individuals whose occupations required them to look ahead and plot trends. They didn't like what they saw on the not-too-distant horizon.

Canadian citizens were selling vast acreages of cottage land to recreation-seeking neighbours to the south. Canadian mining and lumbering firms were selling immense quantities of natural resources for processing in the United States, creating jobs there rather than in the country of their origin. Hundreds of American firms were establishing branch plants and offices in Canada and tying these to American parent firms so securely that major decisions about Canadian operations were being made outside the country.

Canadian culture, they saw too, was dominated by American curricula in books, by American magazines and movies, radio and television networks. Many trade unions in Canada were dominated by their American counterparts.

These and other trends so alarmed the luncheon group that they decided to take some action in stirring up other leading Canadians who were known to share the same concern, and in stirring up Canadians in general.

The trio and their subsequent collaborators in several provinces recognized that the broad situation they were concerned about was not deliberate encroachment. It was not part of a master-mind political plot by a larger adjoining country, but a natural-enough expansion of private interests.[1] The concerned group knew they ran the risk, in sounding off about their concern, of being considered anti-American and even of being called hate-mongers.

What the group needed, as an executive director, was somebody not anti-American in sentiment, but strongly Canadian, highly concerned and a good organizer, who would become spokesman for them. Edwin Goodman, a former national organizer for the Progressive Conservative party and now a member of the concerned group, knew exactly where to lay hands on such a person. He offered to contact Flora MacDonald.

The group had to weigh carefully Flora's Tory stance before endorsing Goodman's recruiting mission, for they wanted to appeal to Canadians irrespective of political parties. Yet they recognized that whoever was recruited as director would belong to some party; they themselves were party men, of more than one kind. Flora MacDonald was a Tory, but not one of the rabid kind who couldn't be trusted with a non-partisan assignment. She was already working in a non-partisan framework in the political studies department at her university.

The arguments Goodman used to enlist some of Flora's "spare time" tied in with her own convictions. So Flora took on another job. On a partial leave of absence from Queen's University, she stumped the country from one side to the other. She spelled out the message in detail, sold memberships and created local chapters of the Committee.[2]

That year was a rough one for Flora in personal terms. Early in 1971, she lost her father, to whom she had been devoted all her life, only a week after she began working with the Committee. Her sister Helen died two months later.

One of Miss MacDonald's CIC recruits, Robert Page, was on his way to becoming a professor in Canadian history at Trent University. He

110

later became national chairman of the Committee for an Independent Canada. He told the present writer how he was won to the cause. "Flora's involvement in the organization drew me in," he said. Flora signed him up for a $5 membership on the floor of Maple Leaf Gardens during the Ontario PC leadership convention in the winter of 1971. By that time he was teaching at Trent and Flora talked him into starting a Peterborough chapter.

"I was impressed with her organizational ability and her enthusiasm. She did a terrific job as the original executive director of the CIC. Her trips into the Maritimes got the organization off the ground. She knew a great many people across the country and that was a great help to her." According to Page, Flora MacDonald's image, even at that time, was of a broad-minded, rather than a narrow, Tory. "She was recognized as a thinking Tory, a Tory prepared to criticize her own breed. This was a distinct advantage in a key position in what was a multi-party organization."

With the help of a research assistant and a secretary, both provided by the Committee, Flora explored in depth the basic thesis of American takeover, helped prepare a statement of purpose, expanded the original newsletter,[3] created pamphlets, produced news releases, gave interviews to newspapers and magazines, and appeared on radio and television programs, including talk shows. She spoke to men's service clubs, women's organizations, youth groups, school classes — anybody who would listen.

A published interview by Lynn Jones, news service editor of the Kingston *Whig-Standard*, gave the gist of the MacDonald message. She talked about the "erosion of Canada's independence by default" rather than by deliberate "sell-out" to American interests, he said. Flora told Mr. Jones that in her speaking tours she urged Canadian citizens to press their members of Parliament for legislation that would "significantly diminish" the influence of outside powers on Canadian life. In particular, she urged the setting up of a federal agency which would "supervise the conduct of foreign-controlled operations in Canada." She told the interviewer that at that time (February 1971) 8,500 Canadian firms were foreign-owned and controlled.

The interviewer asked if her committee wasn't in fact anti-American. She was most emphatic, he said, in stating that the committee was pro-Canadian rather than anti-American. What Flora Mac-Donald wants, he said, is "a Canada that will develop to become the greatest country in the world."

111

"What irks her is the realization that loss of economic control inevitably leads to erosion of Canada's political independence. She mentioned that intrusions by the United States in Canadian political affairs in such things as U.S. insistence on falling in line with its policy of 'no trading with the enemy,' assumed, of course, that the enemy as far as the U.S. is concerned must automatically be the enemy of Canada. A classic example of this occurred some years ago when Ford of Canada won an order to supply vehicles to Red China only to have the order cancelled at U.S. government insistence." Flora is realistic enough to welcome foreign investment, the interviewer said, but it has to be "on Canadian terms."

Research in the areas of CIC concern proved of value to Flora later in her campaign for election to Parliament. Canadian independence became a strong plank in her platform and continued to be a concern she voiced in the House of Commons.

As a postscript to the above, it should be said that at this writing (1976) the Committee for an Independent Canada is still active. It claims a lobby in Parliament of about thirty MPs, who have helped create a new climate of opinion and in some cases legislation on foreign investment, foreign land ownership, Canadian content in education materials, Canadian radio and television, and Canadian periodicals and book publishing.

---

[1] "The astonishing thing about our absorption is its accidental quality, and the way in which we work to bring it about." (Walter Stewart, *Shrug: Trudeau in Power*, p. 133.)

[2] Eventually there were 10,000 members in 50 chapters, including one in Flora's Kingston community.

[3] Eventually it became a little magazine called *The Independencer*.

23
Abroad with forty men

Back in 1947, when the National Defence College was established at Kingston, it would have been close to heresy to propose admitting a woman. Female units had been accepted in the armed services and there were training courses for them. But the defence college was a cut well above service schools. Located at the prestigious and almost three-hundred-year-old site of Fort Frontenac, the college was a graduate-level school for senior officers and policy makers — a school for experts. And the assumption was that all experts are men.

But in a quarter century the social climate had changed. Women had invaded every segment of life, from blacksmithing and embalming to politics, the judge's bench and the headship of nations. So why not a woman at the National Defence College? The idea became lodged somewhere in the upper echelons of the Ministry of National Defence, the ultimate authority for the college. Perhaps in the year marking the quarter-century anniversary of the college, a woman might be admitted, if a suitable one could be found.

The established method of selecting approximately thirty members for each year's eleven-month course — a majority from the military sector and a minority from government services, university, the church and industry — was nomination by one's seniors and approval by a selection committee.

Flora MacDonald had already visited the college as an invited lecturer in Canadian politics. She was highly respected for her knowledge of actual, as against theoretical, workings of political powers

113

and governments. She had shown up well in discussion periods following formal presentations. Her nomination by her university for the 1971-1972 session would have been natural enough if she had been a man. And since the college was prepared to break with tradition, where could the selection committee do better?

For Flora, the opportunity to capture another "first" was attractive. The chance to engage in a year of study midway in her career, particularly a study of the economies, political systems, strategies and problems of other nations, as well as of Canada, was too good to resist. And the fact that a good deal of travel would be involved made it a must.

The fact that she was to be the one woman in a heretofore male program led her to go over to the college ahead of time and talk to the commandant, Rear Admiral S. Mathwin Davis, about any regulations she should particularly be aware of.

He looked at her in her beautifully tailored pantsuit, which she had bought for the occasion, to be as inconspicuous as possible and to be suitably attired for roughing it in travel. His mind leaped to a long-standing regulation at the officers' mess. It wasn't written, of course, to apply to course members, for the assumption was that these would be men. It was meant to apply to any "lady guests" that course members might bring to the dining room. According to the regulation, which pre-dated the fashion of women's pantsuits, the female guests were to be dressed as ladies, not in men's trousers or slacks. The commandant jokingly referred to the regulation, which thereafter was changed to suit the times. Meanwhile, Flora came to the mess hall suitably attired.

Two apocryphal stories have circulated about the little incident. One is to the effect that when Flora was gently told about the regulation forbidding pants she offered to wear only the top! The other story is that a new regulation was posted underneath the original one. It said: "For the purposes of Fort Frontenac Officers' Mess, Flora MacDonald is not to be considered a lady." Though neither story is true, they make for conversation.

Admiral Davis said Flora was a keen student, and both in her formal presentations of research and in discussion periods, though often she obviously knew more about the subject than those presenting it, "she showed admirable restraint."

The year's work was divided as usual between academic presentations and field trips to many parts of the world, for firsthand observation and information. The academic portion consisted in part of forty-five-minute lectures by visiting experts from a variety of fields

114

— military, government, labour, religion, industry — followed by a coffee break and then ninety minutes of discussion.

For other academic inputs, the course members were divided into groups called syndicates. Each syndicate was given a problem to research with the help of the library facility — one of the best in Canada, consisting of 50,000 books and 180 regular magazines and newspapers. When the problem had been defined, explored and discussed by the group, it was presented, along with a proposed solution, to the total group, and there it was subjected to scrutiny and often fierce attack. It had to be defended.

The study areas covered the range of Canadian domestic and international affairs, exploring the country's economic and social development and its relations with other nations — in fact, all matters that help to influence the formulation of policy.

The male members of the course had no other commitments during the year, but Miss MacDonald still carried a reduced work load at the university. She dispatched this in after-hours and on weekends, without apparently affecting the quality of her work at the Defence College.

The field trips, arranged by Transport Command, meant flights from Trenton air base (sixty miles from Kingston) to many parts of the world. The trips, interspersed with series of academic exercises, involved flights to all capitals of Canadian provinces and territories, to New York and Washington, and to many cities of the world. The list of places visited by members of Course 25 reads like a railway time-table. Besides the capitals and New York (scene of the United Nations) they were: Jamaica, Venezuela, Japan, South Korea, Hong Kong, Thailand, Iran, Ethiopia, Kenya, Nigeria, Tunisia, Yugoslavia, Belgium, Germany, Britain, France, Finland and Russia.

At each flight stop, the group was met by representatives of the province, territory or country, given accommodation and often entertained in style. In foreign countries the course members were guests of the Canadian Embassy. Formal sessions were held for the sharing of information.

The commandant, who travelled with the group, tells about something that happened at one of the provincial stops, which he chooses not to name. It was a wretched night late in October when the Hercules cargo aircraft containing the group creaked to a stop and let the passengers alight.

"Sloshing along toward the terminal, I heard the strains of a lone piper, and took the music for a lament on the weather. Inside the terminal, however, all was warm and cheery. The provincial premier was there, which was a pleasant surprise because we weren't to meet him until the next day. I sought to remonstrate with the great man, saying this was a magnificent gesture, but considering the night it hadn't been necessary for him to meet us." According to the admiral, the premier looked slightly embarrassed. "Oh," he said, "I haven't come to meet you — I've come to meet Flora!"

The commandant said this meeting became something of a pattern. "Wherever we went during a year of considerable travel, in Canada, the United States, in Europe and around the world, there was invariably someone, often several somebodies who had just come to meet Flora, and with whom, in faraway places, she left an impression of Canada."

Her fellow traveller added this: "I have rarely met any individual with a greater capacity to absorb and to cherish new experiences. Most of us, even in relatively short travels, tend to become, in Winston Churchill's phrase, 'saturated and satiated with feelings of emotion and sensation,' but not Flora. For her, life and the multitude of varied experiences it has to offer are cherished, and remain cherished month after month and year after year. Perhaps it is this enthusiasm and comprehension that make her so significant a politician."

The commandant tossed in another observation, this one related to a night of entertainment in Moscow, when the group was taken to a nightclub, where the guests, if they so chose, could dance. Flora, as the one woman in the Canadian group, was led on to the floor by the tall, distinguished-looking British Foreign Office member of the course. The music was an old-fashioned waltz. The two swept around the room in professional ballroom style, while one by one other dancing couples dropped out to admire. Flora, caught up in the dance, was unaware that she and her partner were the sole objects of attention. She was in another world.

Back in Kingston, at the end of the course, because this was the quarter-century class, something commemorative had obviously to be done to mark the occasion. A special gingko tree, representing the ancient wisdom of China, was planted in an ornamental garden on the grounds at Fort Frontenac. By common male consent Flora was given the honours of doing the actual planting. The inscription indicates that the tree was planted in 1972 by Flora MacDonald, the first woman to attend the college, within four months of her entering federal Parliament.

Part Five

Member of Parliament

24

A clean contest and a clean sweep

As early as 1968 — before Flora had been two years in Kingston — she had considered running for a seat of her own in the House of Commons, but just when she was weighing the pros and cons, Mr. Stanfield asked her to travel with him and his campaign party in his own 1968 election. Without hesitation, Flora opted for helping the new party leader. She knew she could enter the lists at Kingston at another time.

She had to wait four years for her chance. Meanwhile, she was chalking up still more experience in the political studies department at the university. She was broadening her reading, sharpening her definitions and discussing practical politics. In this four-year interval came the last of her work (until March 1969) as the party's national secretary; she declined to seek re-election on grounds of being too busy. In the same period came her work for the Committee for an Independent Canada and, perhaps most valuable of all, her year of intensive policy study and travel as a course member of the National Defence College.

The riding of Kingston and the Islands had been held by the Liberals for a decade. The incumbent was now Edgar J. Benson, finance minister in the Trudeau government. Flora knew it wouldn't be easy to unseat a minister with political clout, but she also knew that local as well as national feeling against Benson was running strong. People everywhere, including Kingston, were ready to blame him personally for high inflation and national unemployment levels.

119

With her political ear to the ground, Flora MacDonald sensed as well that there was a good deal of complacency within Benson's riding association. This, and her own organizational experience, told her she stood a good chance of returning Sir John A. Macdonald's old riding to the Conservatives.

When, as the riding association's vice-president, she prepared to offer herself for federal nomination in 1972, she wasn't exactly in the mood to take on the world, but she was certainly in the mood to take on Mr. Benson. The staid old riding had never had a woman candidate before, although it had plenty of female election workers. Flora MacDonald was on her way now to try to capture another first: The first woman PC national secretary, the first executive director of the Committee for an Independent Canada, the first woman student at the National Defence College now became the first woman in the Kingston riding to seek a seat in Parliament.

Among those from whom she received help was George Perlin, a member of the political studies department at Queen's University. "The first problem we had to face," said Perlin, "was within the party itself, because Flora was a relatively controversial figure preparing to offer herself for nomination." She had one special advantage. She had made friends and impressed people outside the party. There were many dissatisfied Liberals, New Democrats and people with no political associations or leanings who were potential recruits.

It wasn't a case of going out and recruiting, wholesale, a bunch of strays. Rather it was a case of making it possible for persons in the academic community and elsewhere, who shared her concerns for little and forgotten people and for a government that would be in touch, to identify with her. This grassroots approach was not only the strong part of the campaign, but it became characteristic of all Flora's future campaigning, including that for the party leadership.

There had been speculation, prior to the March 29 nomination meeting, that Valorie Swain, able and popular mayor of Kingston from 1968 to 1972, who had provincial involvements as well as municipal, might press on now for a federal seat. He decided, however, to remain out of contention.

By the time Flora had an ever-growing number of card-carrying enthusiasts ready to go before a nomination meeting, the outcome was predictable. Bogart Trumpour, who had been the last federal Conservative candidate and edged out by Mr. Benson, was on good terms with Flora. But he wanted one more fling of his own at the federal nomination. Flora asked him to nominate her. He said,

"Flora, if I don't run against you, I will nominate you." He let his name be presented with hers and made it a competition.

He found he was running against a popular and skilled political operator, whose roots, even in the short time she had been in Kingston, were in the university, the military, the prison system, the hospitals and several branches of the performing arts. There was hardly a segment of life, from child care to conservation, that Flora Mac-Donald hadn't penetrated. As early as October 1971 *Chatelaine* magazine named her as one of 105 Canadian women the magazine considered should run for Parliament.

Mr. Trumpour hadn't a chance. The meeting was packed with close to a thousand Tories whose minds were made up. Among the crowd was a solid phalanx of women of the community, many of them recruited by long-time Conservatives Audrey McFarlane and Edna Barrett. Defeated in the nomination, Trumpour swung behind Flora and became chairman of a campaign committee which effectively brought together people with specialist knowledge and skills, whom Flora could recruit through her friendships outside the party, local people with hard-headed practical political experience and enthusiastic volunteers attracted to a campaign for the first time by Flora's personality and commitment.

The overall aim was very simple: give the likeable Flora MacDonald all the visibility possible. Strategists came up with the campaign slogan BE IN TOUCH and gave it the two meanings of being in touch with Flora and putting her in Ottawa where she would be in touch with the powers that be on behalf of the people. Flora used every opportunity given her by schools, churches, clubs, youth groups, military, academic and other organizations to show her genuine concern for people and to take shots at the Trudeau government for its neglect.

By the first of September, when the election date was announced, Mr. Benson had gone to another job as president of the Canadian Transport Commission. Flora expressed her disappointment. "He was the one I wanted to beat," she told the press.

According to the local newspaper, Flora blasted the Liberals in Ottawa for their "massive failure of democratic leadership." The government had its chance to "pull Canada together . . . but it failed the challenge and dashed our hopes. . . . Ottawa's technocrats have no feeling for the lives they are playing with so casually, and the people are divided from one another." She faulted the Liberals for spending four years reviewing Canada's constitution — "tearing the document to shreds," but not offering anything new to replace it.

Finally, in September, her opponents appeared on the scene. The Liberals' choice was Dr. John Hazlett, a surgeon. Lars Thompson, a Queen's University education professor, was the choice of the New Democrats. The forty-six-year-old "Red Tory," as some journalists called Flora — a veteran by now of twenty-nine election campaigns on behalf of other political candidates — took them on enthusiastically.

It was reported on every hand that she fought clean. To a reporter who asked her when she was going to get down to a personal campaign against her opponents, she replied: "I don't really think one has to tear one's opponents apart. I think what the electorate expects of me is a clear outline of my position and my potential contributions."

Flora kept hammering away at the Liberal government's indifference to unemployment, high prices and taxes, and at the creeping trend toward foreign control of Canada, which she called "the world's most valuable piece of real estate." She was one of only four candidates from Ontario who were endorsed by the Federation of Ontario Naturalists as being worthy of wholehearted support on environment and conservation grounds.

Young people attracted to Flora and her organization canvassed from door to door. Instead of telling people what Miss MacDonald was promising to do for them, they asked people what they wanted her to do for them. They conveyed the responses, and these were carefully tabulated and echoed in Flora's speeches and campaign literature.

Flora attracted to herself a number of former NDP supporters who were unhappy with the effects of the extremist Waffle movement on that party and were satisfied that Miss MacDonald's position was more nearly their own. One of these was Lynn Jones, former NDP riding treasurer and bagman and for ten years a member of the riding executive.

Hearing that he had broken with the association, Flora made an appointment with him at his home and invited him to join her campaign. "I didn't hesitate and found no conflict between my brand of socialism and Flora's outlook," he said.

Mr. Jones's action and his reasons for it were featured in a CBC documentary called "Take 30", in which Mr. Jones, news service editor of *The Whig-Standard*, related how a number of Queen's professors who had been his NDP colleagues had also quit and offered to work for Miss MacDonald.

"My particular role in that election was a sort of aide-de-camp. I took her on visits to industrial plants, the penitentiaries, coffee parties and the like," he said. "In all these visits one sensed immediately her charm, her acceptability and her remarkable knowledge of a wide range of subjects. Although she was asked tough questions, she was never stumped and usually gave convincing and laudable answers."

Some of her campaign workers came up with a theme song, "Hello, Flora!" adapted from "Hello, Dolly!" in a popular stage production. People broke out singing it on some occasions when the candidate appeared in public.

As her campaign progressed, her pace was intensified. A *Whig-Standard* reporter who spent some time with her said a day with Flora MacDonald was "perpetual motion": handshakes offered everywhere; dashes down various streets to chat with construction workers; waves of recognition from passing motorists who would honk and yell, "Go, Flora, go!"; a lunchtime discussion with fifteen employees, and later in the same lunch hour, conversation with university students.

Someone yells from across the street, "Sock it to 'em, Flora!" At 2 p.m. she is at a new store opening several miles away, shaking hands with customers, listening and responding. From there it is a two-hour session with students, and then a two-hour break to write a speech. At 8 p.m. she speaks at an all-candidates' meeting at the Steelworkers' Hall, and then roars off to talk to a group of homemakers. A few minutes to midnight she says, "I must break off now — a friend has promised to shampoo and set my hair. It's the one chance I'll get before the weekend."[1]

Conservative federal party leader Robert Stanfield was featured in a Kingston campaign rally. So were New Brunswick Premier Richard Hatfield and Eddie Goodman, former national party chairman and one of the leaders of the Committee for an Independent Canada. Michael Martin, an Independent member of the Newfoundland Legislature, whom Flora had helped in the cause of island fishermen, came from St. John's to help Flora in the final week. He used a former connection with the armed services to gain contact with voters on the military base.

During the final weeks of the campaign, no fewer than eight news-gathering sources and magazines scanned the progress of the local campaign. Camera crews from several television stations, in Kingston, Toronto and Ottawa, followed the Kingston campaign at intervals, and so did metropolitan newspapers, as well the ever-present Kingston *Whig-Standard*.

There was general recognition that this was not just an event in Sir John A. Macdonald's old riding and not just a contest involving a woman. There was already speculation that Flora MacDonald might go beyond a back-bencher's seat in the Commons. If the Tories should win, she would be cabinet material, some said. Others let their enthusiasms carry them further. They said she could even be Canada's first woman prime minister.

Flora's mother came from North Sydney to provide a mother's care in the last weeks of the campaign. At 7:15 every morning Mum would serve breakfast — sometimes oatmeal porridge, sometimes orange juice, two boiled eggs, honey on toast, and perked coffee. Often meals had to be served on a tray in front of the telephone, while Flora continued her relentless crusade to win voters. "I often gave her custards or milkshakes at noon — something that digests easily for these tense days," Mum said understandingly.

On election day, sisters Jean and Sheila came the 170 miles from Toronto to Kingston, with their husbands and older children, to be present for the wind-up, whether a victory or defeat. The Mac-Donalds are a close-knit family.

To get out of the public gaze as election day wore on and to compare notes on the day's proceedings, Flora had dinner for herself and two campaign workers, Mike Martin and George Perlin, sent to a motel room. The polls had closed at 7 o'clock. The group thought they would have a leisurely hour before checking on election results. At 7:40, about halfway through the meal, a nervous Perlin went out and made a check on results up to that time. Minutes later he burst into the room, shouting, "You've won, Flora!"

Flora rose slowly, as though in a daze. Her eyes were wide and she whispered hoarsely: "What do you mean?"

"You're leading by three thousand votes," Perlin said.

The results continued to pour in. The final count was 22,820 for Flora MacDonald, 14,094 for Dr. Hazlett, and 5,848 for Lars Thompson. It was the biggest victory ever recorded in the riding.

[1] Sterling Taylor, *The Whig-Standard*, Oct. 20, 1972.

25
On the floor of the Commons

Flora MacDonald had moved her "things," as she called her clothes, typewriter and a few household effects, many times in the twenty-three years she had been bouncing around since leaving her North Sydney home in 1949. Her move to Ottawa after the 1972 election topped all the other moves in significance and complication.

She was a member of Parliament. She could scarcely believe it. The girl who had felt sorry for herself as she rode the bus to business college, who was going into a backwater (she thought) while her classmates were going on — she was an MP now. The girl who had been booted out of Ottawa (as one journalist put it) was returning, right under the nose of the man who had, although indirectly, done the booting.

The move was as frightening as it was gratifying. She had always been nervous on going to a new job — whether at the branch banks in North Sydney, Peterborough and Toronto; at the Selfridge Club in London; at Brock's in Montreal; at the lumber company office in Vancouver; at the PC national headquarters in Ottawa; or at Queen's University. Just thinking of walking onto the floor of the House of Commons, not as a visitor but as a member, set her heart racing and made it hard for her to collect her thoughts.

Her possessions had now to be divided up three ways: some papers and mementos to Room 222, the office assigned to her in the West Block of the Parliament Buildings; some household effects to a newly located apartment in the capital city; and some left in the apartment she would retain in Kingston. The latter, in her constituency, would still be her home, and she would gravitate there on most weekends.

Very soon she would have to reshuffle some of her possessions again, this time to a constituency office somewhere in Kingston. She meant to honour her election promise to keep in touch. Keeping in touch meant having office space, preferably a store front, downtown where people could easily find her on Saturdays.

Somehow, with assistance from friends, relatives and paid help, Flora got it all sorted out. She surveyed the brass sign on her Ottawa office door with satisfaction: FLORA MacDONALD, MP. Yes, she had come a long way. But she couldn't indulge in a feeling that she had arrived at a roosting place. She was here because she had seen tasks to be done. She must get at them.

Her mind had been in a turmoil not only over personal adjustments but over the implications of the situation for the party. True, she had won a personal victory, but the party had lost. The margin was so slim it was maddening: the Tories were only two seats behind the Liberals. She had grieved inwardly for weeks for Mr. Stanfield. He had missed the chief prize — the overthrow of the Liberal government — for the second time. The count in seats was Liberal 109, Progressive Conservative 107, NDP 31, Social Credit 16 and Independent 2.

A minority government again. This meant the Liberals could be turned out on the first non-confidence vote. Then what? Another election could be called within weeks of the opening of the new Parliament. How would she fare then? Horrible thought: elected in October, moving into the House of Commons for a session expected to begin in January, and then having to go through an election all over again!

Of course there was the other alternative: in the event of a Liberal defeat, her party might be asked to form a government. What a scramble there would be in that case, with the Conservative Party not yet healed of its old wounds. What juggling there would be for position. Would she be given a cabinet post? Surely not over members with House experience. But so many of these had been defeated. Some rookies would have to move up fast, and she was hardly a rookie. But if the Conservatives formed a government, they would be subject to the same hazard: they could go down on the first vote!

The new session opened January 4, 1973. And somehow Flora survived opening ceremonies in the Commons, the summons to attend in the Senate chamber, the traditional march through the corridor, the crowding with other MPs into the Senate to hear the Speech

126

Flora MacDonald, MP

Flora talks with
Mr. Stanfield, the leader
of her party from 1967 to 1976.

from the Throne, the return to the Commons and the tabling there of the throne speech, to be debated in the days ahead. Flora wallowed happily in the traditional pageantry and trappings. She was a very proper MP among MPs being very proper. But in the corridor afterward she was the old Flora, greeting friends "loved long since and lost awhile," swapping quips and reminders of headquarters days a decade ago, meeting other newcomers, exchanging good wishes. "Today it's tea and hors d'oeuvres — tomorrow I must get to work," she told her old boss, Senator Grosart.

She lost no time in coming up with her maiden speech in the House, exactly one week after the 29th Parliament opened. It was beautifully timed and a model of public utterance, holding in balance elements of warmth and wit, positive principle and a dash of criticism that may well have told Prime Minister Trudeau and his Liberal cohorts that they could expect more of the same in the days ahead.

In that speech she was another MacDonald, speaking for Sir John A. Macdonald's former riding, on Sir John A's birthday, January 11. Lingering over her opening reference to Sir John, and leaving an unspoken hint that she could be counted on to do homework before speaking, Flora mentioned the somewhat remarkable fact that several MPs present had all been born on Sir John A's birthday: James McGrath, Tom Bell, John Lundrigan and Claude Lachance. The fact that the members congratulated belonged to different parties was an unspoken suggestion that below men's diversities there may often be found a fact of unity.

Reference to Kingston led her to bring in the name of the city's founder, Count Frontenac — a Frenchman, to balance the reference to a Britisher, the Roman Catholic over against the Protestant, all of this being merely hinted rather than openly stated. It was clever. If the House could read the message, it was being told that in this new MP was someone who cared about unity — a united party, including disillusioned Quebec, and if members wanted to read it that way, a united Canada, too.

"What Frontenac in his time, and Macdonald in his, built on this continent they had to defend against military threat, political intrigue and the scepticism or the selfishness of men whose vision was small. Frontenac in the seventeenth century and Macdonald in the nineteenth had ambitions for Canada that transcended the times they lived in and the territory they occupied. Both men looked west. Frontenac extended the power of the king of France into the heart of North America. Macdonald's breathtaking concept of achievement was to secure half the continent to hand on to succeeding generations of Canadians."

Doubling back to the other Macdonald a few seconds later, and referring to the national policy for which he is everywhere remembered, Flora credited the House with the pursuit of "a new national policy." It must have the same "cornerstone" Sir John gave it: "a partnership between English- and French-speaking Canadians." The fact that Canadians "have not reached a lasting solution in the partnership" makes it "imperative for each to find a mode of life with and alongside the other, while at the same time not so weakening the joint enterprise as to lay it open to further erosions of Canada's independence of action — economically, culturally, diplomatically — in relation to its powerful southern neighbour."

She recognized discontent and called for consultation. Having named the partnership of French and English, she brought in the companion fact of "the developing multiculturalism of Canada." And having made that reference, the logical step in the speech was to go directly to the claim on Canada of her native peoples. (Flora was not neglecting her newly assigned portfolio.[1])

Warming to her subject, Miss MacDonald spoke of the "moral redress Canadians owe those they have so shamefully treated in the past." The throne speech, she said, was "shockingly inadequate — in fact abysmally silent" on this subject. "There was not a single word about the native peoples." The nature of native problems "requires [action], our past neglect imposes it, and the human suffering and injustice involved cry out for it." For one who had not been formally schooled in Greek and Roman rhetoric, Flora was showing skilful use of it.

In the first ten minutes Flora had tucked a great deal into that maiden speech. For the next ten she expanded her earlier reference to Canadian independence. Picking up the Macdonald thread again, she said Sir John A. wanted a strong independent state. "In that sense, too, I am a nationalist," she said. And now she spelled out the items she had dealt with from coast to coast when she stumped the country for the Committee for an Independent Canada.

A new national policy, she insisted, must commit Canada to the elimination of poverty, the reduction of unemployment, the control of soaring food prices and, very important, the building again of strong political parties and their earning again of the confidence of the public.

That was on January 11. Another eleven days and she was back with a searching major speech scoring on the government for merely fiddling around with another long-term study on world trends in food prices. Studying, always studying, and not acting, while "almost one-third of the population of our country live on or below the poverty line," she charged.

Another year-long study, just released, she said, tries to persuade people that they are really getting a bargain at food stores. "What a bargain indeed!" she said cynically. "Is this government . . . so callous and so insensitive it can tell all those on fixed incomes what a bargain they are getting as food prices increase? I really do wonder whether the minister would be prepared to meet concerned Canadians like customers, people on welfare, old age pensioners, the working poor, 615,000 unemployed, all those on fixed incomes, to tell them what a bargain they are getting?"

"It is cold comfort to a woman on a widow's allowance to be told by the Minister of Agriculture she is getting a bargain in food prices. It is cold comfort to a mother eking out a living on a mother's allowance to be told a food inquiry will eventually provide answers to her current needs. It is cold comfort, indeed, to an old age pensioner to be told his pension will be increased some time before April, perhaps, while food prices go up day by day."

Miss MacDonald pleaded for action now — not just another study which could end up a long time hence in an empty flour bin. "With fuzzily defined terms of reference and a committee report at some unspecified date, the minister seems hell-bent on taking his time," she charged.

Much of Flora's performance in the House during her first session had to do with her office as Conservative critic of Indian and Northern Affairs in Opposition Leader Robert Stanfield's "shadow cabinet."[2] But the member for Kingston and the Islands made use of question periods to direct queries on subjects like amendment of the British North America Act, capital punishment, a proposed energy conference, a finance conference, immigration, income tax, high school dropouts, mercury contamination, youth programs, Mackenzie Highway expenditures, arctic transportation and penitentiary and parole matters.

James McGrath, the MP who shared a desk with Miss MacDonald during her first five months in the House, said she "never asked frivolous questions," and "always showed she was well prepared." At times he doubted the value of packing so much information into a question; he felt it was better to keep the "enemy" in the dark about how much one knows. But he credited Flora with being, even in her first session, well on the way to becoming a skilled parliamentarian.

McGrath admits he was inadvertently the cause of getting Flora rattled one day when she caught the Speaker's eye and rose to ask a question on Indian affairs. Mistakenly thinking his desk microphone was turned off, he whispered to her, "Sock it to them, Flora baby!" All hell broke loose. The Conservatives gave her a round of desk-thumping applause which lasted several minutes. When it finally died down, a blushing Flora put her question and the proceedings resumed.

Miss MacDonald's background of over six years in Kingston and specific work there within the federal penitentiary system led her to speak out for reform in services involving five institutions, two thousand inmates and fifteen hundred employees. She urged a parliamentary committee, which was then giving some attention to prison administration, to work for improved communication between different levels of the penitentiary service — local, regional and national. She called for new programs for inmates and an examination of the guard-prisoner relationship. She raised questions about the adequacy of psychiatric facilities and complained about mediocre education facilities in the Prison for Women. "The committee," she said too, "should press for less secrecy and more openness on the part of the penitentiary system, an openness that is free of distortion and distrust."

Mr. McGrath said he was impressed with the way Flora stood up to criticism. "She's had enough criticism aimed at her over the years that she knows how to let it roll off her back."

[1] See Chapter 26.
[2] *Ibid.*

26
One of Bob's bird dogs

The shadow cabinet appointed by Opposition Leader Robert Stanfield at the beginning of the 29th Parliament had a double purpose. If
the Liberal minority government should fall early, the Conservatives
would have a working structure in readiness. Mr. Stanfield doubtless
hoped that the mere fact of having such a structure would encourage
the Governor-General, in the event of a Liberal collapse, to call on the
Tories to take over — a perfectly legal procedure, which had some
precedent. Meanwhile, the device of the shadow cabinet would give
the opposition an effective method of bird-dogging all members of
the government cabinet.

True to election-time predictions, Flora MacDonald was considered
cabinet material. Stanfield recognized Flora's concern for minority
groups and asked the new member to interest herself in Indian Affairs and Northern Development. This pleased Flora more than, say,
an assignment to Health and Welfare, which might have been considered appropriate to the supposed domestic interests of a woman
member.

George Manuel, president of the National Indian Brotherhood,
had already been to Mr. Stanfield to express his concern that whoever
was appointed to the Indian portfolio be fully sympathetic to the
recently awakened aspirations of Canada's native peoples. Paul Yewchuk, member for Athabasca, had been acting unofficially as critic of
Indian affairs, and had applied himself efficiently. When Mr. Stanfield put in a quiet word about Flora MacDonald's general competence, Manuel was a bit dubious. Yewchuk he knew and trusted. He
didn't know anything about Flora.

132

"Give this member a try," Manuel remembers Stanfield saying. "If you're dissatisfied with her performance, we can talk about it somewhere down the road." Manuel was agreeable, and it was announced the next day that Flora would be Indian critic for the Conservative party.

Manuel said Flora got in touch with him before he had a chance to contact her. She asked if she could meet with him. He suggested she come to the Brotherhood office and meet the staff there. She went over and spent all afternoon. When she left she had the president's complete confidence and the good will of the staff of about thirty-two.

In an interview, executive assistant Marie Marilli said: "I was impressed with her because she didn't come on much like a politician. She was willing to listen and had briefed herself so she didn't ask ignorant questions. She didn't give us her pet theories on Indian affairs, but listened to what we had to say. Her sensitivity and her insight into the issues really impressed me." The assistant went on to say this first impression lasted. "On the occasions I met her she was always very relaxed. She was courteous and attentive and talked to people as her equals; she didn't put up any barriers."

At that first meeting Flora asked Mr. Manuel to get her an invitation to all the meetings of Indian bands. According to the official, Miss MacDonald visited all the native communities across the nation and in a short time was talking to their leaders on a first-name basis.

When Flora was invited to talk to the rather exclusive Empire Club in Toronto about aboriginal rights, she saw that George Manuel and Tony Belcourt, president of the Native Council of Canada, were invited too and that they were given seats with her at the head table. Mr. Manuel said he went rather expecting that in this setting Miss MacDonald would not tackle the aboriginal rights problem head on. "We are such a minority in Canada — only about one and a half per cent," he remarked. But he was "extremely impressed with her performance" both in the speech and in the way she handled the questions that followed.

If Flora can be said to have taken her gloves off before the Empire Club, she took them off and threw them on the floor, figuratively, at the April 11, 1973 afternoon session of the House of Commons, when it seemed likely that the question of aboriginal rights might be brought to a vote.

"Today . . . is the first time this vital matter has been debated in the House . . . as a whole [in contrast to debate in committees], in over a hundred years. . . . The government has failed to recognize the concept of aboriginal rights and has rejected the concept outright," she said, as she plunged into a major speech.[1]

"Previous governments," she said, "may have failed to fulfil their obligations to the hundreds of thousands of Indian people, but they never questioned the principle." Then came the 1969 white paper on Indian policy, in which the minister for Indian Affairs said the land claims were "not realistic."

Alluding to the backing she was receiving in her caucus,[2] she said "the Progressive Conservative party undertakes to settle fairly the outstanding aboriginal claims of Canada's native people. We intend to work toward a negotiated settlement of disputed treaty and aboriginal claims . . . in full and fair consultation with the native people involved."

She went back into history on the North American continent and showed how the concept of aboriginal rights had been recognized by Spain and "later applied in other colonial areas." She read into the parliamentary record the Royal Proclamation of 1763 and the interpretation of Mr. Justice Hall of the Supreme Court, as applying to the Hudson Bay territories, or Rupert's Land, and to the lands west of the continental divide. She maintained that section 91 of the British North America Act made the federal government the trustee for the native rights concept.

Flora maintained that since the issuing of the 1969 white paper, dealings with native peoples had been placed "on the shifting sands of temporary policies and programs which are viewed by the government as gifts which can be given or withheld."

Figuratively speaking, she ripped several inches of skin off the back of Indian Affairs Minister Jean Chrétien for his statements on a national television show. The minister had asked the public to help him form a definition of aboriginal rights. "He made it clear he would like to hear from the other parties. He is hearing from them today," she said. (There were voices of "Hear, hear" heard in the House.) "I find it ludicrous that a man who has been minister of Indian affairs for five years should have to ask for a definition of aboriginal rights. What has he been doing for the last five years, if he hasn't learned that?"

She was glad to note that the government had abandoned the 1969 policy paper, which it had tried to force on the Indian people. But "what we are seeing in the interim is a series of *ad hoc* arrangements with no overall thrust. The government is content to hide behind a smokescreen of individual arrangements. . . . The minister has

134

evaded the issue, avoided, abdicated, skirted around and brushed aside the fact that the government has constitutional responsibility for the James Bay Indians and their claims as aboriginal citizens."[3]

She took up the minister's comment that "if the Indians win . . . the Quebec government will be in a very difficult position." She advised Mr. Chrétien not to spend his time worrying about the position of the provincial government: "It is the federal government which will be in a tough spot trying to justify its action or, more importantly, its inaction."

Flora commended the chairman of the standing committee on Indian affairs, Liberal MP Judd Buchanan (who later succeeded Mr. Chrétien), for stating in London that the federal government should recognize the claims of Canada's aboriginal peoples to lands never ceded to the white man through treaties and that the native people have a moral claim which the government must recognize. "I say he is a credit to his party and his committee," Flora remarked.

She put the alternatives to the Speaker: to continue the present system, which she maintained would make the native people increasingly dependent on a giant bureaucracy which had not produced any long-term solutions; or come to a settlement in principle of native claims, which would "put the relationship of the government and the native peoples on the basis of rights, not charity."

Frank Howard, NDP member from Skeena, pressed the Speaker to call for a vote, rather than let the question slip from its position on the order paper and come then under the authority of government orders. He feared that if the matter went to government orders it could either be brought forward "or buried forever." The House adjourned at 6 p.m. without the question being put. So, as Mr. Howard feared, the matter went back to the government for action — or inaction, as the case turned out.

Mr. Manuel credited Flora MacDonald with a good try. "She challenged the House to vote on the issue but the government refused; they chose to talk it out of the House, which is a strategy the government uses when they don't want to make a decision on anything."

While this one House debate is presented here to illustrate a single issue in Indian affairs, it must not be assumed it was the only issue. During the 29th Parliament Miss MacDonald was criss-crossing the country, visiting native communities, making notes, telephoning, receiving and presenting briefs and dealing with other issues such as mercury pollution, discrimination in employment and the status of Indian women who marry non-Indian men.

She was speaking to native and white audiences, initiating research and, on the basis of the research, asking pertinent questions in the House. She was criticizing in particular the James Bay project for its probable effect on thousands of native people, whose way of life and livelihood would be disturbed. She insisted it was too heavy a price to pay for the creation of mainly surplus power for export to the United States.

An incident related to Indian affairs got a wide airing in the press and in the Commons in September 1973 when some Indian files disappeared from the office of the Department of Indian Affairs and Northern Development. Police officers of the Ottawa city force and the RCMP came into Flora's office without permission and when she was absent — which is against parliamentary regulations. The officers interrogated her staff. When Flora learned over the telephone that they were there she told them to leave and come back when she could be present.

Under parliamentary rules relating to privilege, no one, not even the police, may enter a member's quarters, much less interrogate the persons there, without express permission. The accepted procedure is to inquire at the security desk at the entrance to the building. The security officer asks permission of the member or the member's staff, and until this is gained, the visitor is not entitled to go farther.

The House accepted Flora's statement that she knew nothing about the files and rebuked both police forces for their breach of a member's privileges. Flora considered the settlement of the matter not a personal victory but a victory for the parliamentary system.

In her work in her first portfolio in the shadow cabinet, Flora divided the broad task of Indian Affairs and Northern Development into three sections, each under a subcommittee chairman. One section looked after such needs of native peoples as medicine, education and research on treaty rights. Another concerned itself with development of the north and wrestled with such matters as environment, exploration, construction, the Mackenzie Valley corridor and the James Bay Hydro development. A third, under Joe Clark (Rocky Mountain), concerned itself with national parks.

Miss MacDonald in due course received reports from her sub-chairmen and discussed with them matters of policy, which were then followed up. But now and then, as in the case of aboriginal rights and the James Bay project, Flora involved herself in the specifics. Her office was in constant touch with that of the National Brotherhood and with native councils from coast to coast.

[1] House of Commons Debates (*Hansard*), 1973, Vol. III, p. 3207.
[2] Stanfield made this election promise.
[3] *Op. cit.*, p. 3209.

27

Keeping in touch

"I intend to keep in touch," Flora MacDonald had told her campaign workers and public audiences prior to the 1972 election in Kingston. "Oh, sure," a skeptic mumbled. "It's great campaign talk." Politicians were expected to make promises.

Within weeks of her election, Flora had a Saturday morning radio open-line show underway in Kingston. She was at CKLC radio station in person for each broadcast, responding to a rush of phone calls.

Early in December she launched the second of her "keeping in touch" expedients: a constituency office on Kingston's main street. A full-time young and personable ex-teacher, Darlene Downie, was put in charge, with permission to pull in volunteers to help if the load got too heavy. Flora picked up the expense tab for rent, furniture, office supplies, salary and incidentals — a matter of $10,000, the first charge on her expected salary of $26,000.[1]

The office was open six days a week, and Flora was there much of the time herself until the session began in January. About thirty telephone calls a day were handled in that period and a total of fifteen hundred letters.[2] Fortunately, many of the first letters were messages of congratulation and didn't require a formal answer. But the other kind came too, and typing services had to be arranged to supplement the counselling which the two women were doing by telephone and in office visits.

Problems referred to Miss MacDonald and her staff varied. Many people were vague about which of the three levels of government — municipal, provincial or federal — was the appropriate one for their

138

problem; these callers had simply to be steered in the proper direction. Other callers had complaints about one government level or another; a discreet inquiry and a follow-up phone call or letter took care of the situation.

Many people were confused about unemployment insurance and wanted somebody to put government gobbledygook into plain language. Unemployed persons needed a lead or two and the assurance from somebody they trusted that it was worth trying again. A phone call to the Manpower office would help pave the way for still another interview.[3] Flora tried to help a man who wanted to get into the Ontario Provincial Police. She found he didn't have enough education and sent him a letter to that effect. She received a letter from him telling her to drop dead.

Relatives told Flora about an upcoming golden anniversary, and she touched off congratulatory messages at various political levels. Long-delayed visas and passports were hurried up, usually through contact with Flora's Ottawa office.

Senior citizens phoned or wrote plaintively about rising costs in relation to fixed incomes, or because they were confused about a pension or got on the wrong side of a computer. The working poor complained about gouging landlords, falling ceilings and the need for pest control. Operators of small businesses inquired about loans, and homeowners asked for information about mortgages.

Relatives of prison inmates contacted Flora about prison regulations that restricted visiting hours or to ask her to try to make a personal contact. Health problems, social welfare, hardships through labour strife, school dropouts, noisy neighbours, and dogs that showed signs of frothing at the mouth — all got an airing in the constituency office.

Each inquiry was listed on a form, with space left for information obtained in a follow-up. These files were arranged alphabetically, but were available only to staff persons; confidentiality was respected.

Sometimes people who phoned in would insist on sharing their problem only with Flora. These were given an appointment for a Saturday, for after the Commons session started, she had to limit her personal appearances in the office to that one day. There were times when the appointment book looked like one in the office of a doctor or a dentist.

In the outer office were two bulletin boards with pin-up notices about various government programs and services. Immigration regulations were available in several languages.

In the inner office, where Miss MacDonald met her constituents, were copies of the parliamentary record (*Hansard*) and separate copies of speeches and questions which Flora had voiced in the Commons or elsewhere across the country. The office had its own clipping files for pertinent articles appearing in local and metropolitan newspapers and magazines. Here too were kept organizations' minutes and newsletters, so that the member for Kingston and the Islands would be informed of ongoing events and transactions in the community.

Once the parliamentary session had begun, the weekly radio call-ins were received in Flora's Ottawa office. Soon the MP's travelling schedule threatened to wash out the call-in program, because she couldn't always be in Ottawa for the program hour, which along the way got changed from Saturday to Wednesday. The station and Miss MacDonald worked out an arrangement by which she would conduct her side of the 9:10 to 10 a.m. program from wherever she happened to be on the program morning. It could be as far away as Vancouver or Newfoundland.

To make sure that Flora was kept informed about the local scene, a portfolio of newspaper clippings, resumés of city council, planning board and other meetings, and memos about tragedies and also happy events was sent to her in Ottawa by the end of each week. She would telephone Tuesday night to get the last of the news, so that she would be reasonably well informed when she went on the air from her remote post. All this was what she meant by the policy of keeping in touch, and at this writing it is still going on.

A staff member listens to every call-in program and stands by to provide information. If a phoned-in query calls for some research, Flora has only to say, "I'll have my staff look into this and get in touch with you," and the girls at 324 Princess Street take it from there.

Her keep-in-touch policy means making herself accessible. She has consistently kept the news departments of the area media (the newspapers and radio and television stations) informed of her activities. She has a listed telephone number at her Kingston apartment, although this exposes her to calls at any time of the night when she is trying to get needed sleep. Few crank calls are received, but there are always some. One Christmas morning, following the public furore over increases in federal members' pay, an irate male phoned to say: "I hope you don't get even a single Christmas card — you stingy bitch!" The caller seemed unaware that Flora opposed the pay raise. He was barking up the wrong tree.

The Kingston and Islands member doesn't like abuse any more than other persons, but she considers a certain amount of it inevitable. People do get frustrated and angry. She recognizes, apparently, that in many cases having to do with slow-moving government bureaucracies, it may be for rather good reason.

The Kingston office handles speaking requests originating locally. The staff clears with Flora and with the other office, which does the same for requests outside of Kingston. Between the two offices they make sure appointments are not made for the same date or hour.

Keeping in touch meant meeting with citizen groups and listening to their complaints and suggestions. It meant meeting frequently with university personnel for discussions on policy. Noteworthy in the latter category were Flora's Sunday night discussions at the home of Professor and Mrs. James McCowan. They would have her over for the evening meal and then she and this leading conservationist would talk until near midnight about matters like resource depletion and the need for legislative and regulatory counter action.

They discussed as well problems in Canadian publishing and the effects of the drawoff of Canadian advertising dollars by American magazines — chiefly *Time* and *Reader's Digest*. Immigration was another topic. "On this we could never agree," the professor said. "My view was that we should stabilize our population, which is one component of growth. World population is increasing by seventy-eight million a year, so we couldn't think of even a substantial portion of this increase coming to Canada. Her instincts are against limitation. She thinks of the poor immigrant coming to this country and making good."

The policy of keeping in touch meant, and continues to mean, an immediate service to constituents; it also means Flora is exposed to a climate of opinion which she is able to express in parliamentary committees and in the Commons.

---

[1] Later the government took over much of the expense and Flora handled the rest.
[2] There were 5,000 office contacts in the first year.
[3] A man asked what to do with a government notice which informed him he was dead.

28
Many irons in the fire

When Flora MacDonald had been on Parliament Hill for six months, the Kingston *Whig-Standard* sent a reporter to Ottawa to follow her around for a day. Julie Ages returned almost exhausted and wrote the following.[1]

Room 222, West Block, Parliament Hill. A solid oak door opens on Flora MacDonald, MP for Kingston and the Islands. Room 222 is fast earning the reputation of being the storm centre of the West Block. Does she ever stop, this woman whose life has been politics since the 1950s?

The moment Flora arrives on the Hill at 8 a.m., the stark office begins to hum. First there's a quick call to Darlene Downie, who heads Flora's Kingston constituency office.[2] "What's new in Kingston?" Flora wants to know from Mrs. Downie, an ex-teacher who was smitten with the world of politics during Flora's fight for the Kingston and the Islands seat in the House of Commons.

Next the MP dashes downstairs to eat breakfast in the parliamentary cafeteria. Between spoonfuls of porridge, she engages in a tête-à-tête with fellow MP Heath MacQuarrie, Progressive Conservative critic on health and welfare. They talk about possible snags in passing the old age pension increases bill, slated for that afternoon.

Flora finishes breakfast with a glance at *The Globe and Mail* for George Bain's column and the "Questions in the House" column.

It's Wednesday, the day Flora and Alderman George Webb produce the open-line show on CKLC radio, with Kingston area listeners speaking to their MP direct to Parliament Hill. A caller gets rude with a query about "no good politicians." Flora reacts quietly, explaining her side of things. Listeners say she's never blown her cool on the show.

Flora takes note of every question asked. She tells one caller worried about "the alarming increase in local crime" that she is not afraid to walk down any street in Kingston. To another caller, opposed to the James Bay project, Flora answers: "I am very concerned about a project of this magnitude affecting the environment, people, climate and biology of one-sixth of Quebec. When will the federal government step in and exercise its authority?"

The show over, the unmarried MP puts down the receiver and dials Kay Reed, one of Flora's election campaign assistants. Dress fittings have been arranged in Kingston for the weekend. "Be there at 10:30 Saturday morning," Mrs. Reed advises the red-haired politician, who no longer has time to arrange these things herself.

The office is stark and dreary, with grey walls and dowdy furniture circa World War II. The office used to belong to a Liberal undersecretary, who was later promoted to the cabinet, Robert Stanbury.

Flora's support staff consists of secretary Anne Westall and research assistant Nancy Gilber. Their adjoining office is dominated, from floor to ceiling, by green filing cabinets containing information on everything from the Committee for an Independent Canada, to the PC party, to abortion.

Wednesdays at 10:30 a.m. is PC general caucus time, where policy matters are mulled over by the top Conservative MPs. Caucus ends two and a half hours later, and Flora dashes back to her office for a desk lunch: a peanut butter and jam sandwich, a glass of milk and a chocolate sundae.[3]

On other days, she says, lunch-time is often devoted to delegations from Kingston, school children on their first trip to see how Parliament works, a businessman seeking a hearing, a group of enthusiastic Olympics supporters.

It's 2 p.m. A bell rings, summoning MPs to their seats in the Commons for the afternoon session. For Flora, it's a running dash down a long tunnel connecting the West Block with the Commons. Flora asks a question about Indian affairs. Loud desk-thumping from the Conservative back benches almost drowns out the reply from Jean Chrétien, minister in charge of Indian affairs.

The question period over, Flora disappears through the curtains at the side of the House. It's back through the tunnel and up to her office, where freelance journalist Douglas Kirkaldy is waiting to see her. He's producing a radio documentary on political commentator Charles Lynch. Flora's a close personal friend of the Lynch family, and she tells the interviewer that Mr. Lynch "deals with issues in terms of personalities. They become alive in the eyes of his readers and therefore he achieves a more meaningful relationship with them. In a very chatty, personal way he interprets Parliament."

The journalist leaves. More desk work. The MP includes her business card with a letter; it's signed simply "Flora." This informal touch is part of Flora's political philosophy: be accessible and in touch at all times.

It's 5:30 and quieter now. The civil servants have long since taken their buses and commuter cars home. The bells ring out unexpectedly, calling the politicians back to the House for a surprise vote on the old age pension bill. It's back down through the tunnel to the House.

The voting over, Flora remembers a reception by the Native Council of Canada. She attends, chatting informally with many non-status Indians. She will speak at their banquet the next night.

The day is not over. The MP returns to her office at 8 p.m., has dinner sent up, and begins three hours of dictation into a tape recorder.

"It's the only time I get to really catch up on paper work," she explains somewhat apologetically to the exhausted reporter who's been trailing her.

Whoever said that the life of an MP is one big round of cocktail parties?

*   *   *

On other days, snatches of time not spent in the House might be taken up with such other chores as assigning research and indicating guidelines for it, perusing research reports, reading the parliamentary record and committee minutes, drafting questions for speeches in caucus or in the Commons and preparing speeches to be given in

144

various places across the country, reading lengthy report volumes, holding telephone conversations with fellow MPs, officials at party headquarters or in some riding where party workers wanted to discuss possible techniques for a by-election. Or she might be called to confer with the party's leader, Robert Stanfield. Or she might be taking another lesson in French.

---

[1] Used by permission of *The Whig-Standard*.
[2] Mrs. Downie now has other employment, but she still speaks in glowing terms of her earlier association with Flora MacDonald.
[3] Flora's brother says she would often make a meal on a smoked-meat sandwich and a quart of milk — "that's where she got her energy".

29
One issue, one remedy

Flora MacDonald had been in the 29th Parliament only seventeen months when the minority Liberal government was brought down in May 1974 on a motion over a new budget. The motion, proposed by the New Democrats, was supported by the Conservatives and opposed, without effect, by Social Credit members. All parties were now required to go back to the people for a new mandate. It was a foregone conclusion that the ruling issue across the country would be inflation.

A summer election in Kingston was at the worst of all possible times for a candidate in Flora MacDonald's position. Less than two years before this, she had challenged what had been a predominantly Liberal riding federally — although provincially Conservative. University students had constituted many of her storm troops for door-to-door canvassing and some other campaign jobs. And they had accounted for a good chunk of the vote that had given Flora a landslide victory. With most of the students away, Flora had to get along without an important group of campaign workers and nurse the uncomfortable expectation that her cause would lack at least a couple of thousand votes.

Added to this main problem was a degree of complacency arising from Flora's whopping victory the last time and the general favour she enjoyed as a result of her keep-in-touch policy. People said, "She'll make it again, hands down." Workers excused themselves in batches, although they promised their votes at election time.

Some of this reluctance had to be attributed to the decision at the national level to fight the election on a one-issue, one-remedy

146

strategy: inflation, the issue; wages and price controls, the remedy. In Kingston, as the Tory campaign organization was taking shape, many people grumbled about this platform.

In a situation like this, either you operate within the framework of the policy established by the national leader, or you ignore your leader and focus on local issues. In Flora's case, she genuinely believed there were aspects of wage and price controls that were credible and therefore marketable. She took these and made the most of them. She didn't just pretend to go along as a gesture to party loyalty.

In due time, even the Liberals would come around to imposing controls, which vindicated the Opposition's stance; but of course, that would be much too late to help Conservatives across the country win the 1974 election.

At the Kingston PC nomination meeting in May, Flora was unopposed. She and a guest MP colleague, James McGrath of St. John's East, Newfoundland, came down hard on inflation and stressed the Conservatives' proposed remedy. Flora then went on to other matters, enumerating some of the things she had been working on during the preceding months: an increase in the old age pension, extension of the cutoff deadline for the Veterans' Land Act provisions, increased medical research, equality of opportunity for women, electoral reform, election expenses reform and, above all, Indian and Northern Affairs, which was her portfolio in the shadow cabinet.

At the Liberals' nomination meeting, Peter Watson, a young education professor, was chosen to represent the riding. The NDPs sent Lars Thompson back into the battle. At the Liberals' nomination meeting, Hugh Poulin, the party's member for Ottawa Centre, told delegates and friends that Flora MacDonald would be another "one-term Tory" to be added to the record after the July 8 election.

He said Kingston had a great tradition. A long time ago it was represented by the Conservatives, but for the last forty years it had been Liberal, except for a few times when there had been "aberrations." "You are now starting down the road to eliminating another aberration," he said confidently. He went on to blister Mr. Stanfield and to refer to Dalton Camp and Flora MacDonald as "political Pollyannas," used by Mr. Stanfield to "get rid of Mr. Diefenbaker."

Against such "pleasantries" Kingston Tories launched their campaign. In the absence of university students for door-to-door visitation, the candidates in all parties had to depend largely on group confrontations in meet-the-candidates nights.

Progressive
Conservative
nominating
convention,
May 1974

Flora celebrates a birthday
during the 1974 election campaign.

Flora's family turn out to support her on election day.
The photograph shows Flora's mother (on her left)
and her sisters, Lorna, Jean and Sheila.

Flora makes her
acceptance speech.

One of these, in the Grand Theatre, presented some anxious moments and even a little comedy. A Flora supporter, whose last few stops on the way to the theatre had obviously been at nearby drinking spots, kept interrupting the proceedings with a question. When the chairman kept ruling him out of order, he insisted that Flora be the one to take up his cause. She appreciated his support, but in his condition it wasn't really helping her. The man kept interrupting, and finally the chairman asked the ushers to remove him.

That's where the situation took on an un-funny aspect. As three ushers confronted the man, he said, "You'd better get some more help!" A fight was obviously shaping up at the front of the hall. At this moment, Flora, at her place on the platform, put down her pencil and came down from the platform. The man threw his arms around her in a fond embrace. Flora accepted his affection, and the crowd applauded. A moment later, Flora was walking him down the aisle and the two were chatting like bosom pals. Flora returned within minutes, to a cheering house. She had dealt with the situation without any loss to her prestige or her cause.

On these meet-the-candidates nights, the usual pattern was followed: first an opening statement by each candidate and then questions from the audience. Flora showed up well in the question periods — often better then than in formal speeches, where she was tied to the manuscript before her unless she had taken time to commit her material to memory.

She presented a good appearance and voice on local television programs, and because of her prominence in the party, the fact that she was a woman and the speculation that she might one day offer herself for party leadership, she was frequently interviewed on network programs.

*   *   *

Flora's advertising attacked the issue of inflation. "Something CAN be done to control inflation," she said in the heading for a block advertisement in the local newspaper. This appeared with an attractive head-and-shoulders of the candidate. The piece went on to say: "The Progressive Conservative Party says something CAN be done about inflation in Canada.

"Something CAN be done because three-fifths of the current inflation is produced by factors right here in Canada, conditions in the Canadian economy which can be controlled in Canada.

150

"And something CAN be done because Canada, unlike virtually every other major industrial nation, has the ability to produce all of its own energy, nearly all of its essential food requirements, and most of the basic raw materials we need to maintain a strong industrial economy."

Then came another heading: CANADA MUST END GOVERNMENT-PRODUCED INFLATION. And the copy went on to say: Government has contributed substantially to inflation in Canada through excessive and wasteful spending and conflicting and irrational federal and provincial taxation policies. A Progressive Conservative government is pledged to:

1. Produce a balanced federal budget;
2. Appoint a commission to work out a program of cost efficiencies in federal administration;
3. Cut or eliminate federal sales taxes;
4. Negotiate new tax agreements with the provinces to reduce the inflationary effects of taxation and provide stable economic growth;
5. Develop with the provinces a federal-provincial capital spending policy to ensure orderly capital allocation by government;
6. Co-ordinate the activities of federal departments concerned with economic policy and develop joint economic planning between the federal and provincial governments.

Then another heading: CANADA MUST CONTROL ITS OWN ECONOMY. And another block of copy broken up for easy reading: The central goal of Progressive Conservative policy is long-term price stability with full employment. To achieve this goal Canada must have effective control of its own economy. A Progressive Conservative government, therefore, will:

1. Use a system of incentives to establish Canadian ownership of more than 50% of the non-renewable resource industries in Canada;
2. Use a system of incentives to establish Canadian ownership of at least one major producer in every important sector of our economy;
3. Convene an international conference to establish international agreements for the regulation of the activities of multi-national corporations;
4. Provide government assistance for the development of a strong independent Canadian technological capability.

Then a final heading: A NEW NATIONAL DEVELOPMENT STRATEGY, and more copy: A Progressive Conservative government will initiate and implement a new national development strategy for Canada. Among other things it will —

1. Provide incentives for the processing of Canadian national resources in Canada;
2. Ensure the conservation of Canadian raw materials to meet long-term domestic needs;
3. Establish a national energy policy to conserve energy resources for long-term Canadian needs and to ensure that supplies from domestic sources are available in all parts of Canada at reasonable cost;
4. Undertake measures to increase business competition and strengthen measures to curb abuses by monopolies.

In big letters under all this appeared the name FLORA, and the campaign committee's final pitch: "On July 8, re-elect Flora MacDonald."

Another advertisement, broken down along similar lines, appeared under the heading, WHAT DOES A PRICES AND INCOMES POLICY MEAN TO YOU?

Advertisements like these were too long to be digested by the general public, but they were meaningful to the academic, military, business and professional segments of the community; and the less sophisticated might be expected to suppose Flora knew what she was talking about.

*   *   *

In public meetings she rode hard on Mr. Trudeau but left her local opponents alone. At a meeting in a district hall, she said that in May 1973 a government confidential memo listed inflation as number 6 on a list of Canada's problems, but just the other day Mr. Trudeau promised to fight inflation. "Mr. Trudeau has finally discovered inflation. . . . It took him only four years." She told the audience too that the $120 billion spent since Pierre Trudeau became prime minister in

1968 represented "more than all government spending of the past hundred years." To another audience she described the Prime Minister's leadership as "exhausted, ineffective and indifferent."

One of the problems the campaign organizers had was to keep Flora anchored in Kingston during the campaign; she was forever dashing off to help some other candidate. Two nights before the July 8 election, she was driven to Pembroke, 160 miles away, to speak for the PC candidate there. On the way back to Kingston, late at night, she tried to get a little sleep in the back of a station wagon. Before six o'clock the next morning, the last day of campaigning, some of her workers called for her so she could meet industrial workers at a change of shift. She was kept on the hop all day — speaking here, mainstreeting there — and finally dropped off at her apartment about 6:30 at night.

Her endurance was a byword, but to test her, Fred Madden, one of her workers, said, "Flora, I'm going out for a snack and I'll be back for you in half an hour — we've got the evening to put in yet." According to Mr. Madden, Flora said, "I'll be ready." But Madden threw in the sponge and went home to bed.

The election results showed that despite the absence of the student vote and despite the hard-to-swallow wage and price control remedy and despite the trend across the country, which swept the Liberals back to power with a majority government (140 seats to the Tories 95 seats), Flora MacDonald had polled 17,795 votes in her riding.[1] She was the only PC woman candidate who made it.

[1] Peter Watson received 13,957 and Lars Thompson, 6,874.

30
Boning up

The 30th Parliament — Flora's second — got underway on September 30, 1974, with the usual ceremonies. The Liberal government now had 141 seats in the 264-seat Commons, so there was no chance, as before, of its being dumped prior to the next called election. The election should be about 1978.

Since the government had the numerical strength now to plow through, if necessary, on what it saw to be major problems, Flora MacDonald faulted it for not dealing more forthrightly, in the Speech from the Throne, with Canada's number one problem, inflation.

"To the astonishment of most members, even his most ardent backbench supporters, the Prime Minister in his one-and-a-half-hour speech [read by Chief Justice Bora Laskin in the absence of Governor-General Jules Leger, who was recuperating from a stroke] never once touched on the economic difficulties that face so many Canadians, particularly those on lower and fixed incomes," Flora wrote in the hometown weekly.[1] She said he tagged the subject of inflation on as the last of a list of things to be discussed in the new term in the House.

A Canadian Press story said that some of the promises made by Trudeau during the election campaign would not be dealt with immediately. "Government officials say they were intended to be carried out during the life of the new majority Parliament, expected to last at least four years."

Two months after the new session opened, Flora was given a new portfolio, that of critic of Housing and Urban Affairs — a post formerly handled by Eldon Woolliams of Calgary North. Her old post in

154

the shadow cabinet was split in two: Indian Affairs went to Dr. J. R. Holmes of Lambeth-Kent, and Northern Affairs went to Douglas Neil of Moose Jaw.

Miss MacDonald's headship of the new Conservative caucus committee meant a great deal of homework, especially on the technical side of construction and mortgages. But Flora had extra supplies of smoked-meat sandwiches and quarts of milk brought to her desk, where she waded through relevant parliamentary acts, regulations, committee minutes and new research memoranda. In other hours she had conferences with key people. Tom Sloan, senior assistant with Opposition Leader Stanfield, said of Flora: "She's the hardest worker we've ever had." Boning up also meant poring over a lot of materials at her Kingston apartment during the Christmas recess.

Early in January she was ready to accuse the government of failing to come to grips with the housing situation in Canada. Figures released by the Central Mortgage and Housing Corporation indicated housing starts were 46 per cent lower in December 1974 than in December 1973. Flora predicted acute shortages in 1975, unless the government, which she said had been "depending primarily on patchwork programs," acted immediately.

Hers wasn't the only voice calling for action in the housing field. "There has been a developing squeeze in money market conditions," wrote a Montreal columnist, Bruce Whitestone. "Mirroring that shortage, interest rates have been rising, curtailing the supply of loans of all kinds, but particularly mortgage credit. . . . Mortgage rates are now at stratospheric levels, more than 12 per cent. . . . A high level of house building will depend on efforts to control inflation."[2]

A week later, following a meeting of provincial housing ministers with federal housing minister Barney Danson, Lorne Nicholson, in British Columbia, said the federal $1.4 billion 1975 housing budget for CMHC was "in effect a 20 per cent decline from 1974 because of increased interest costs." Ontario's minister, Donald Irvine, said he was convinced the federal government just didn't give a damn. Mr. Danson countered that the government aimed at producing a minimum of 210,000 housing units in 1975. By July Flora MacDonald would be pointing out that the government was 50,000 units short.[3]

Too little, too late, Flora said as early as February, as she predicted that "Canada is well on the way to a major housing crisis. . . . Economists anticipate that only 180,000 units will be built in 1975, whereas the Economic Council of Canada states that over 250,000 units are required to meet the most basic needs of the country."[4]

On her committee's urging, the Conservatives pressed the government to ensure that large amounts of money would be available for low-cost mortgages. "Without this, all the rest amounts to rhetoric," Flora said. She commended the government, however, for a new Registered Home Ownership Saving Program, which allowed a person who didn't own a home to place up to $1,000 a year in a special account and deduct the amount from taxable income.

In May, she said in the House: "I am told that in some markets at least, unless conditions improve, housing prices will rise by at least 15 per cent within a year. That is hardly a pleasant prospect for a country in which housing prices are already far too high for many thousands of its citizens. Housing prices will in fact have a double impact on inflation. Not only will the price of housing increase but more pressure will be put on wage and salary earners to demand even higher increases to meet escalating costs for this largest single item in the family budget."[5]

In the same speech she predicted mortgage rates of 12 per cent before the end of 1975. "In a very real sense . . . these rising mortgage rates mean that Canadians in their housing budgets are being asked to bear the financial brunt of the international balance of payments difficulties now facing the government . . . the government is forced to maintain interest rates at a very high level in order to attract short-term flows of foreign capital. Whether that is a proper policy from a balance of payments point of view is one question, but there is no question that this high interest rate policy is a disaster as far as Canadian housing needs are concerned . . . as far as the housing crisis is concerned, this government simply has made no response."

In July, the housing critic proposed four measures designed to meet the current housing crisis head-on:

1. Meet the high interest problem by making mortgage payments above 8 per cent tax deductible to a maximum of $1,000 a year;
2. Increase housing starts by subsidizing mortgages to the rate of 8 per cent, with the subsidies payable on the first $30,000 of mortgage financing;
3. Increase the supply of mortgage funds by providing an investment tax credit for money invested in housing mortgages;
4. Increase the supply of serviced land through a fund to municipalities so they can install sewer and water services for new subdivisions.

The $275 million which such a program would require could be obtained by "reordering the priorities of government spending," Miss MacDonald said.[6]

Among scores of items dealt with in the 1974 and 1975 sessions of the Commons — many of which brought Flora MacDonald to her feet, if only to ask another of her searching questions — was one of a somewhat delicate nature, hanging over from the 29th Parliament. It was a government bill originally proposing a 50 per cent salary increase for federal members. A storm of public criticism had led the government to shelve the bill until after the Christmas recess. It was then brought back in the watered-down form of a one-third pay raise.

Miss MacDonald had said, prior to Christmas, that she agreed that a pay raise in some amount was needed, but she couldn't agree to the 50 per cent proposed. She was using $4,000 of her salary to subsidize her constituency office and a large sum for travel. She could well use another staff member in her Ottawa office to handle matters related to her shadow cabinet role.

But the bill, she said, had been badly timed; the government had brought it in when it was talking about constraints in spending. Moreover, it would have been better to have a formula worked out by an independent commission so that members could receive periodic salary increases, the same as in other sectors of society, instead of having a hassle over pay increases every four or eight years.

She made a further point: "Society should ask itself what it considers to be the worth of a member of Parliament in relation to other professions — doctors, lawyers, university professors and so on. Are we saying they are not worth as much? Or are we saying we want only people who are wealthy (and can subsidize their incomes) or people who work at the job only part time, while earning at other things?"[7]

When the bill in its new form was put to the House, it was approved by a 175 to 25 vote. Members' basic salaries were increased from $18,000 to $24,000, with an added tax-free allowance for expenses. Flora was one of the small minority voting against the increase. (Mr. Diefenbaker was another.) "At a time when government was preaching restraint it wasn't setting an example I could follow, in asking for a 33⅓ per cent increase," she said.

She repeated her former stand that the decision should not have been foisted on the members but should have been given to an independent body. Nor did she find an across-the-board and the same-for-everybody method a fair one. "I think someone should look at the inequities in MP's expenses. The member for the Northwest Territories, for example, has a pass to travel between Ottawa and Yellowknife, but once he is there he must cover his own expenses to travel through a 1.3 million square mile constituency. In contrast, a member in a downtown Toronto riding is connected to people in his constituency by a 35-cent subway fare," she said.

With two offices, two homes and a car to keep up, along with a wardrobe, travel, accommodation, election and other expenses, Flora MacDonald has no trouble spending all her salary.

Curiously, just because she is a public figure and an attractive single woman, Flora has had to field frequent questions from newsmen about her private life. She has always had many escorts. Has she had any lovers, they want to know. What about affairs? Why hasn't she married?

To the last question she has a couple of stock answers. "I never got around to asking anyone," is one answer. If the questioner is a known bachelor, she may laugh and say, "Are you asking me?" The other stock answer is to say she *is* married — to her work. And not having any other husband saves her a lot of problems. If she can't sleep, she can turn on the light and read, with no questions asked. If she decides to remain at the office, she doesn't have to account to anyone at home. Her mother says Flora has never given any of her admirers enough of her time to encourage him to think he could pry her away from her first love, which is politics.

The rather puzzling thing for strangers who have heard about Flora MacDonald as a career woman is that when they get around to meeting her they find she is not, as they may have suspected, a hard-bitten and aloof spinster type; she is genuinely close and affectionate — everybody's sister.

[1] *Kingston News*, Oct. 9, 1974. (The paper has since been discontinued.)
[2] *The Whig-Standard*, Jan. 22, 1975.
[3] *Hansard*, Vol. 119, Number 163, p. 7184.
[4] The year ended, however, with a surprising 231,000 starts, according to the March 6, 1976, *Financial Post*.
[5] *Hansard*, number cited, p. 6060.
[6] *Ibid.*, pp. 7186, 7187.
[7] Quoted by *The Whig-Standard*, Dec. 16, 1974.

31

There's more in the cupboard

In presenting excerpts from speeches Flora MacDonald has given across the country since she became a member of Parliament, one runs the risk of being slightly unfair. An excerpt is an excerpt and not the whole speech. And even a single speech is a mere slice from the loaf of one's total thoughts on a given subject.

But an excerpt is better than nothing. The reader will just have to grant that Flora had more to say on these subjects than is presented here. But at the same time the reader can assume that the more, while it may fill out the subject, is not likely to contradict the excerpt.

A second comment seems necessary. When a parliamentarian gets as far up the ladder as Flora MacDonald, research assistants and speechwriters become necessary. How then can one be sure Flora herself said these things? One can be as sure as the fact that she commissioned the research, gave guidelines for it, reviewed it, discussed it and amended the speech based on it so that it would be her style of utterance rather than somebody else's. Who wrote the original draft matters little. Flora worked it over until it said what she wanted to say.

WOMEN IN POLITICS

We are still inclined to think of women in politics as a new phenomenon, even though it has been half a century since Agnes Macphail was first elected to the Canadian Parliament. Surely by

159

now the novelty, the curiosity about women in politics should have passed. . . . But why are there not more women in politics?

Some suggest that the answer is to be found in the attitudes of the electorate. I question that assumption. Before I sought the Conservative nomination in Kingston and the Islands I did a study to determine the resistance of voters to a woman candidate. Most people had no very strong feelings one way or another and would vote as readily for a woman as for a man.

Others feel that political parties themselves are the obstacle. Recruitment of women as candidates has never had high priority. . . .

What is most important is the attitudes of women themselves to careers in politics. . . . Women have been reluctant for personal, occupational and financial reasons to step into the political arena. . . . Confidence then surely is the key. Confidence to take on responsibility. Confidence to challenge men on equal grounds. Confidence to handle any job, covering the whole political gambit from making sandwiches and coffee, participating in policy-making and organizational positions, to running as candidates. . . .

Women must recognize that politics is a profession. Like other professions, political office requires training, disciplined study and a period of active apprenticeship. Election to office does not happen accidentally. It entails involvement in and mastery of an increasingly scientific process. Women must have the confidence and determination to follow this route through to its logical conclusion — election to office.

The trend is there. In 1968 there was one women in the House of Commons. Two elections later, women's representation had increased ninefold. At this rate of increase we can anticipate eighty-one women MPs by the early 1980s!

It is imperative in order to achieve real equality that women prove their credibility to handle any issue — resource development, finance, urban growth, Dominion-provincial relations, economic affairs. . . .

— From an address to a Zonta club

On another occasion, Miss MacDonald said:

Women have made some of their deepest incursions into the political field. . . . We may "have come a long way, baby," but we have a long way yet to go. We may be walking the corridors of political power, but we have yet to populate the inner sanctums where major, nation-shaping decisions are made. . . . There is no significant input by women into the major political or corporate wielding of real power. . . . Much of the fault is our own. . . . Imbued with a Florence Nightingale complex, most women seek to serve those who exercise power rather than to wield it. Instead, women, having served as apprentices to the powerful, must now seek in their own right to gain top-level positions.

— From an address on International Women's Year 1975

WHAT IS A NATIONALIST?

In a sense I have impeccable credentials as a Canadian nationalist. As a MacDonald representing the federal riding of Kingston and the Islands, I have a powerful tradition to maintain and a great example to follow. John Dales, the economic historian, has written of my predecessor: "Sir John A. Macdonald gave us our first national policy and our first lesson in the irrelevance of economics. . . . Macdonald was the first great Canadian non-economist."

I don't think that this is the time or the place to attempt to develop a full definition of nationalism, but I do think I should tell you at the outset something about the sort of stable that the hobby horse I ride calls home. My fundamental postulate is rather simple and I think indisputable by any reasonable Canadian: what I want is to ensure that Canada, as a social, economic, political and cultural entity, establish now and maintain always in the future the right and the power to decide for herself what is best for herself and her people.

It is not always possible to program one's collective destiny for generations ahead. The environment within which we operate is continually changing and our values and wants evolve through time. Thus it is not sufficient to have some latitude for action now; it is essential to ensure ourselves that we shall have in the future the power and freedom to act, to adjust our direction according to circumstances and in line with our deep-seated convictions.

We are often faced with what our friends the economists refer to as a trade-off between short-run benefits and longer-run benefits. . . . My central concern is that we should not allow things that are expedient now in dealing with economic, social and political issues to foreclose important options or to diminish the flexibility and latitude Canadians will have in making policy decisions in the

161

Flora is made a patron of the St. Andrew's Society of Kingston, November 1974

Attending a Grade II presentation at the Canadian Forces Base in Baden-Solingen, Germany

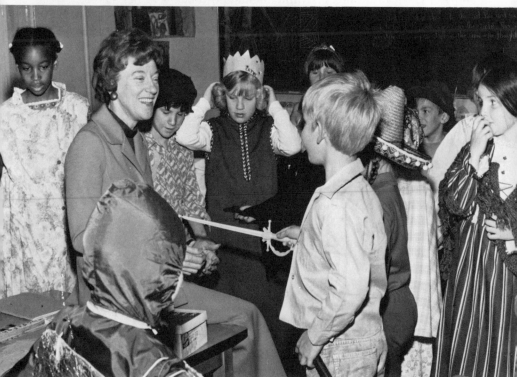

Young people from across the country attend the Rotary Club's Adventure in Citizenship week. Flora attends a picnic for the 1975 group.

A display of Eskimo carvings for the residents at the Canadian National Institute for the Blind

future. I'm a firm believer in the nationalist's commandment: "Do not unto future generations what you would not have had done unto you."

— From a speech to the Canadian Manufacturers' Association

ECONOMIC GROWTH

It must be clear to all of us by now that the time is fast approaching, if indeed it is not already here, when we must face up four-square to this issue of growth itself, this mentality which has taught us to express human worth almost entirely in economic terms. We now have had it brought home to us in the starkest terms that the pursuit of growth and consumption simply cannot go on endlessly, for the very elementary reason that we do not have endless resources with which to fuel and sustain such growth and consumption.

But one wonders whether, even if this delusion of endless resources had not been so resoundingly shattered, we might not have been forced, in any event, to reconsider the usefulness and implications of our growth philosophy in social terms. For surely this overpowering drive to consume, this promotion of materialism to the neglect of our moral and spiritual dimensions as humans, has been a prime factor in encouraging our absence of self-restraint and our lack of any clear sense of broad social responsibility. We have been taught to take all we can get, partly at least on the basis of the mistaken notion that there still could be enough left for everyone else.

Now we are learning, in vivid terms, that this simply is not so, and we are increasingly frustrated and concerned by the implications of that elemental fact of life. If the pit is not endless, how do we measure and establish the limits on what is there? If we can no longer use the supposed laws of supply and demand to justify a kind of each-for-himself philosophy, what kind of alternate process can we establish to apportion our increasingly scarce resources among us? If growth itself is no longer ample justification, what are to be the new yardsticks and the new mechanisms?

Again, of course, there are no easy answers, although I do believe that at least some of the possible alternatives are becoming clearer to us. We still have, for example, one resource — our human resource — far short of full utilization. There are some 800,000

164

unemployed persons in this country right now who bear witness to that, not to mention the countless others whose skills and talents and energies are terribly underemployed. And so we can continue our move toward a more service-oriented economy which emphasizes this renewable human resource rather than consuming our scarce non-renewable assets. . . .

— From a speech to Grocery Products Manufacturers of Canada

NOTIONS OF "RIGHT" AND "LEFT"

In the context of economic growth some people cry out for the systems of extremism. To some it is the extreme of socialism, the simplicity of belief that in total concentration of power in the state lies our salvation. To others it is the opposite extreme, a demand that we return to the unrestricted private enterprise of nineteenth-century liberalism with its glorification of individual laissez-faire.

Surely we know that these are truly the impossible dreams. . . . The simplistic notions of "right" and "left" . . . are misleading and dangerous, misleading because they are emotional terms, all too capable of arousing passions and provoking the kind of conflict which can threaten the stability of our political and social order. . . . There may well be a temptation among some in the political process to play upon the fears and frustrations of so many in our society with simplistic and emotional sloganeering. I can think of nothing more dangerous than that a political party — or we as a society — fall prey to such sirens.

— From an address to a university women's club

HUMANISTIC CAPITALISM

Personally I look to an economic system in Canada that is unique, since it will be tailored to our own needs. The role of the private sector is vital. I have never believed, as do some nationalists, that state control is essential to ensure the collective will is implemented. The collective will is expressed in all sectors. I look to the Canadian private sector to develop an approach, an ethos, an ethic that could be called a humanistic capitalism.

There absolutely must be a recognition that business and industrial activity cannot be reduced to simple mercenary considerations. The French have a term I like very much. They refer to "les

165

chevaliers d'industrie." Maybe it is time that we started to talk about and serve an economic chivalry.

We need to develop a new approach to the concept of accountability. No longer can we be satisfied with a view of ourselves and our country that leaves each Canadian accountable only to himself and his conscience. The magnitude of the challenges before us demands that each sector reassess its role. Businessmen, no less than politicians, must recognize their moral responsibility to each other and to future generations. It is in your hands to help promote social efficiency through social responsibility.

— From a speech to The Canadian Manufacturers' Association

CANADIAN RESOURCE POLICY

There are those who . . . prefer to assume that new fuel discoveries will emerge to sustain the next generation. Perhaps they will, but it is reckless to rely on that assumption. I am a Conservative, and I do not believe in taking such massive gambles with another generation's well-being. I believe that our own living should be so conducted that our children and their children could enjoy our way of life indefinitely. Our policies must be sustainable in the north and everywhere else. We must not sacrifice the resources we have to one last futile extension of the wasteful practices now followed by ourselves or our neighbour to the south.

— From an address to social science teachers

BEING A CONSERVATIVE

I am a Conservative. As a Conservative, I believe . . . that freedom can only be achieved within a framework of social order. That means . . . focusing our attention on society as a whole, not on any one part of it, but on all of its parts in relation to one another. It means that increasingly the main responsibility of political leadership must be to sponsor and sustain that process of defining and articulating our collective values and goals.

Conversely, less and less can the role of political leadership in this society be to offer specific answers to specific questions. The post-industrial society is too complicated, its needs are too sophisticated to permit any leader to understand all of its problems, let alone to find solutions to them. We live now in an era where expert knowledge is needed in the production and application of almost every piece of public policy. The role of political leadership in this kind of society cannot be to provide directly that amount of required expertise. It can and should be to translate the choices provided by the experts into language the community can understand. . . .

— From a speech to Grocery Products Manufacturers of Canada

POLITICAL ALIENATION

Political alienation is one of the characteristics of our evolution toward post-industrial society. . . . The individual has come to feel helpless before the power and insensitivity of both public and private bureaucracies. . . . Our challenge is not to destroy bureaucracy, but to control it. . . . Bureaucratic power must be made responsive to the collective interest of the community, whether it is the bureaucratic power of great trade unions, the bureaucratic power of great corporations, or the bureaucratic power of governments.

— From an address to the Society of Broadcast Executives

INFLATION

What are some of the implications for our society of continuing high levels of inflation? While there are many, I want to stress two. First, there will be an increase in tension. It is well known that during periods of inflation all citizens are not able to protect themselves in an equal fashion. The powerful, well-organized members of society are able to make adjustments to new conditions, but others cannot. The consequence is that those who can organize do so simply as a matter of protection. It is not astonishing in the face of the inflation of the last two years that hospital workers, teachers, nurses and many other groups have unionized so that they can exert their power as a group, rather than as individuals, when negotiating wage contracts . . . it is not surprising that there has been an increase in strikes, since they are a manifestation of power against power. . . .

Secondly, the inevitable result of inflation is that groups turn to government for help in solving their problems. . . . If one believes, as I do, that increased government intervention in the economy and society is not what the majority of Canadians want, then the nature of our dilemma is clear: inflation will continue, and it will lead to more government participation, but this is precisely what we do not want. . . . Government must intrude less, not more, in the lives of people. It must spend, not more, but less. It must do, not more, but less if it is to be responsible to what people really want in our society today. . . .

In this country, I believe there is a yearning for order and responsibility. There is a need for a new set of priorities, with less emphasis on government but more effectiveness by government in its areas of responsibility. . . . We are entering a difficult period when growth will not be automatic, where everyone cannot automatically have more, where reward will have to be related more closely to contribution and where government must reassess its role in the economy and society.

—From an address to businessmen

INEFFECTIVE LIBERAL LEADERSHIP

A year ago the Liberals were successful in persuading the country that price and income controls were both unnecessary and bad. By doing this the government succeeded in designating inflation as a problem of only secondary official importance.

Then after a typical pause — and the Liberal style seems to be characterized by lengthy pauses broken by erratic bursts of activity — the minister of finance became concerned about inflation and undertook a brief series of talks with leaders in various sectors to see if there was a consensus to undertake a program of self-restraint. It is little wonder that his approach didn't work at that time. The government had already said it was against controls. It had demonstrated in the clearest way that it had no intention of taking action on its own.

It did nothing to curb its own programs and expenditures. It did nothing to give incentives to business and to increase productivity to help keep prices down. It raised interest rates to the point where new investment became virtually unfeasible and where price increases were almost inevitable just to finance inventories. It ran up an unprecedented deficit.

It increased its own and its civil service salaries and expanded the size of the civil service itself. It defended rising food prices. It raised the price of oil and gasoline and put a new tax on them. It made a mess of its own labour relations, and, by both action and example, created out of the whole collective bargaining system in Canada a chaotic situation unparalleled in our history.

The search for consensus was quickly abandoned. And more time went by. Then suddenly, out of the blue, a program was introduced that promised control for some and relative immunity for others. What a way to mobilize national support for one of the most important pieces of peacetime legislation in our history. Whether the government will be able to accomplish its objectives after that sort of preparation, only time will tell. But if it fails, the reasons are not difficult to find.

There had been no political preparation for this announcement, no attempt to gain public support for what the government had previously and quite recently told the people was bad and unnecessary. There was no leadership by example, no application of the kind of restraint that was now being urged on the country. There was only the federal presence we've come to expect at certain crisis points in our life as a nation: the glittery-eyed television performer, balefully staring down the opposition, stonily deaf to the unanswered questions, coldly imposing his will on the people.

I, as a Canadian, have a right to expect more from my government. I have a right to expect some leadership, some example. It is just not good enough to be dictated to by people who are there to serve me, particularly when their actions belie their own commitments.

This, I call a failure of leadership.

— *From an address to the Empire Club of Canada*

QUEBEC

Even if it were possible to achieve national victory without substantial support in a province that contains more than a quarter of the voters of the country, I would not ignore Quebec. I don't want a party that is like the Liberal party — one that is not fully and truly representative of all parts of this land. . . .

By and large, the people of Quebec want the same things as do the people of the Prairies [where Flora was speaking]. They want

169

an end to inflation, they want stable prices. They want a sound, diversified economy that will provide employment for themselves and for their children. They want to be assured of the continuing economic existence of their towns and villages. They want commercial policies that will encourage exports. They want a sure supply of energy at the best possible price. They want social stability — an end to disorder in the streets, an end to organized crime, and an end to disorganized government. They want adequate housing at prices and on terms they can afford.

In brief, they want the same things as the people in Winnipeg or Estevan or Medicine Hat or Edmonton. They want good government — honest government and just government.

— From an address to the Women's Canadian Club

HIGHER EDUCATION

The so-called "paper chase" is being strongly attacked on two fronts: for its failure to educate the young either for life or for making a living. Perhaps that's because we've developed a set of unreal expectations about what schools should do for us. . . . Ideally, your time in school will have taught you to ask lots of questions. Almost certainly it won't — and shouldn't — have given you all the answers. . . .

I hope you won't make the mistake which has been made by many of the generations which preceded you: that of confusing schooling with learning. One is a process which is part of life, with a beginning and an end. The other is a process which is life. It begins at the moment of birth itself and should never come to an end as long as life goes on.

Just consider the number of options open to you, the infinite catalogue of opportunities for learning which are within your reach: travel, art in all its branches, community involvement, professional growth and development, to name just a few. Take advantage of all of them, if you possibly can! Because the day will surely come when it will seem to you that the time is all too short in which to absorb all the richness of experience in this world.

The purpose of education . . . is not merely to discipline and instruct but above all to free the mind: to free it from the darkness, the narrowness, the groundless fears and self-defeating passions of ignorance. . . . A free mind insists on seeking out reality, and reality is often a far more painful matter than the soft and comfortable illusions of the intellectually poor. . . .

In the light of a truly free mind, no prejudice can disguise itself as zeal; no bullying can masquerade as leadership; no pettiness can pose as importance. The truly freed mind will not confuse a sentimentality with a true emotion, an act of violence with an act of heroism, or a slogan with a cause.

Men and women with freed minds may often be mistaken, but they are seldom fooled. They may be influenced, but they are not intimidated. They may be perplexed, but they will never be completely lost.

— From an address to a college graduation class

INTERNATIONALISM

Over the years one can detect some slight shift from parochialism to regionalism, and even to a slight Canadianism, but no real spirit of internationalism has emerged. After one hundred years we are slowly becoming citizens of Canada rather than Cape Bretoners or North Winnipeggers, but there is little or no effort to assume our individual responsibilities as citizens of the world. Here we sit, the fortunate real estate owners of the most favoured, most blessed nation on earth, and yet we continue to be inward-looking, introspective, isolationist, bemused by our own problems, absorbed in our parochial disputes, begrudging expenditures on foreign aid while millions starve.

It would have a salutary effect on this country if all Canadians could be exposed, as I have been recently, to the monumental problems of a country like India, whose population has increased by 110 million in the last six years; or as some of our newsmen have been exposed to the indescribable tragedies resulting from the Biafran-Nigerian conflict. We might change from introverts to internationalists overnight.

— From an address after returning from a visit to India

MY DREAM FOR CANADA

To survive in Canada we must develop Canada, and to develop Canada we must build the industrial, resource, transportation,

171

communications and energy structure appropriate to the needs of a strong and viable nation.

Its method of execution is basic: we end our preoccupation with the economy of the United States and our fear of the international financial situation, but we work and build and achieve on our own; we fear not how or whether we must attract outside capital, but develop our own financial structures; we worry not as much about what others say as we do about developing confidence of our own, a truly Canadian confidence.

It is a one-Canada concept, sweeping across our vast country. It is sustained by our great resources, in which all regions share, to which all regions contribute their skills, productivity, imagination, income.

It is based on an economy of stability, unafraid of doing effective battle with inflation, recession and unemployment.

It is cemented by a Confederation in which all Canadians have the respect of all other Canadians and the dignity of all cultures.

It is made efficient by a working co-ordination of federal and provincial authorities designed to implement common goals for the common good.

It is administered by a government of competence, even excellence, that can consult and act to set priorities and provide perspective.

It is, above all, a Canada where people may aspire to a truly worthwhile life; a nation not of oppressive regulation, but of opportunity; a nation not of limited ambition, but of unparalleled achievement; a nation not of pockets of poverty, but of adequate prosperity; a nation not of the common denominator, but of the human being; a nation not of divided factions, but of affection for constituent groups; a nation like none other. A nation that is our own.

I am a Canadian. I've not had any desire to be anything else. My dream is of and for Canada. It is a great country with great people. I feel fortunate to have lived in all sections of Canada, travelled to many places, met with many, many Canadians. I feel fortunate, but I do not feel complacent because I know it is incumbent on me to stretch my potential to its fullest in the service of this country and of my own dream of its future greatness.

— From a speech at a John A. Macdonald dinner

Part Six
Candidate for Party Leadership

32
Needed: a winner

The big question in Canadian federal politics in 1974 was who would succeed Robert Stanfield when he announced that he was stepping down as Opposition Leader. The successor could well expect to face Liberal Prime Minister Pierre Elliott Trudeau in the next election. Barring a crisis that would overturn the government, this would be in 1978.

Stanfield had failed three times to turn the trick against the wily and articulate Trudeau (1968, 1972 and 1974). His failures had been added to two by John Diefenbaker, in 1963 and 1965. The Tories had now lost five elections in twelve years, and the failure syndrome was apparent; the situation was getting desperate. The party simply had to come up with a sure winner. By the powers given to it by its constitution, the national association called for a leadership convention for February 1976.

Flora MacDonald was once asked in Halifax when it was that she first contemplated entering the leadership race. She answered candidly that for her to enter politics at all, which she had done in 1972, was to consider leadership a possibility. Her drive from earliest school days had always been to come first. "I must stretch my potential to the fullest," she keeps telling school groups. This being so, it was a case of timing — timing mixed with the consideration one owed one's colleagues who might have similar ambitions.[1]

While Stanfield waited and waited for the appropriate moment to set a date for the leadership convention, Flora parried all inquiries by old friends and an eager press. A veritable spate of speculative magazine and newspaper feature articles appeared, and Flora was involved in endless radio and television interviews. Even before her formal entry into the leadership race, she was much sought after as a public speaker and was often introduced as the likely next prime minister.

The entire press wasn't behind her, of course. Her old colleague Dalton Camp said in his *Toronto Star* column in January 1975 that Flora hadn't a chance, for the simple reason that she was a woman in what was traditionally a man's game. And a single woman at that! The public finds itself more comfortable with married women, Camp said. He admitted in an interview with *The Whig-Standard* that Miss MacDonald was highly competent, but he said the major segments of society — the resource industries, agriculture, fisheries, trade unions and what-not — are dominated by men, "who wouldn't know how to relate to a woman."

Flora and women across the country were furious over this putdown. What bothered Flora most was that Mr. Camp still looked on her as the Girl Friday with the green notebook who did little chores for everybody. "He doesn't credit me with learning anything in the last ten years; this is completely unfair," she said.

Mr. Camp notwithstanding, when Margaret Thatcher won the leadership of the British Conservative party a month later, the calls for Miss MacDonald's entry into the Canadian leadership race became more insistent than ever. "It's a great encouragement to the rest of us. It indicates that there is no position in the party to which a woman cannot aspire," she said, guardedly. She noted, however, that there is one big difference between the British and Canadian methods of choosing a party leader. It is the caucus in Britain — some 260 Conservative members of Parliament at present — who choose one of themselves, but in Canada the choice is on a much broader base. Ten times that number of delegates, only a small proportion of whom are parliamentarians, make the choice.

In August of 1975, Stanfield made it final; he would not seek to succeed himself. Flora knew the way was now open for her if she wanted to take it. But she is a very astute politician. She had to know the risks a woman would take in such a race. She couldn't afford to be foolhardy, to be considered a weirdo or some kind of kook in what was then International Women's Year.

Her advisers, including Eddie Goodman, agreed she had better test still further the general feeling in Canada toward a woman leader, and in particular the feeling of the party. Accordingly, Miss

MacDonald did a quick swing through key Canadian cities — on a friendly speaking tour.

She was persuaded the time was ripe. She should take the plunge. Pointing in the same direction was a poll taken by the Canadian Institute of Public Opinion. It indicated that 73 per cent of Canadians would not be swayed in their support of a political party if the latter nominated a woman as its federal leader.

One method had paid off for Flora in her two elections to Parliament. Get in early and wear down the prejudice against a woman, and make up for resistance by sheer hard work and good strategy. Let the public see you and hear you. This would mean a long campaign and therefore an expensive one. She would have to rack up thousands of miles of travel and large hotel bills, not to mention contracting for other expensive items. Her backers gave her the green light.

It was now October 1975. She would like to have been the first to announce a candidacy, but in this chance for another first she had already been robbed by Heward Grafftey, member for the Quebec riding of Brome-Missisquoi. He had made his announcement the year before, following Mr. Stanfield's statement that he was stepping down.[2]

On October 8, Flora made her long-looked-for announcement at an Ottawa press conference. "I'm a candidate with a difference," she told the reporters. And she proceeded to spell out the differences. "I am a woman. I represent no single region. I'm neither a lawyer, nor a business executive, nor an academic," she said, tacitly recognizing that all these things could be held against her. She was prepared to swim against the stream. She said her campaign would have two broad aims. She would seek to return government to the people and to give them a sense of purpose and achievement to replace their cynicism and despair of a bureaucracy gone mad.

Her campaign organization, on the basis of thirty-eight earlier campaigns, had been quietly taking shape for two months and was now unwrapped. Her executive assistant was Michael Vaughan, and her campaign manager was Terry O'Connor, an Oakville, Ontario, lawyer who had held the federal seat for Halton riding from 1972 to 1974. Eddie Goodman was made fund-raiser. Hugh Hanson, of Toronto, with a background in federal as well as provincial civil services, co-ordinated policy statements worked up by a network of researchers across the country. Murray Coolican became tour manager.

Delegate contacts were established in all major cities, and special contacts for youth's and women's organizations. Fulltime staff — some paid and some, at their own insistence, on a volunteer basis — numbered about thirty, and as the convention date approached, the volunteers swelled to almost three hundred.

The inexperience of many was offset by a catching enthusiasm and held in check where necessary by experienced decision makers. The Flora MacDonald machine was smooth and effective. Shuttling back and forth across the vast spaces in Canada, again and again, by plane (regularly scheduled service), train, automobile, bus and, for a few short hops, by a helicopter owned by a supporter, Flora kept in touch with her organization, and her organization put her in touch with some 220 out of 264 ridings and their delegates.

The common pattern followed was to invite all delegates in an area to converge at one meeting place, where they had a chance to meet Flora in person, hear her in a formal statement of policy and ask questions. In predominantly French communities, Flora spoke in French and responded in either French or English, depending on which language was used by the questioner. Delegate meetings were interspersed with major fund-raising events in Toronto and Kingston.

Early in the campaign, Mr. Goodman, with Flora's endorsement, established a grassroots fund which he called "Five to Fifty for Flora," meaning $5 minimum to $50 maximum for campaign expenses. According to her financial agent, $40,000 was raised in this way.

When it was found that most gifts were from men, a special appeal went out for women to become personally involved, with one-dollar gifts as a token of their interest and personal support. "Literally thousands of $1 and $2 bills ... poured into Flora's House of Commons office, some with scribbled notes. One included a supermarket bonus coupon."[3]

A week before the convention, Flora opened her books on her campaign financing, and included the names of all contributors who gave more than $100. She challenged the other candidates to make similar declarations. Up to February 10, $103,480 had been contributed by so-called "little people." More than 95 per cent gave amounts of less than $50, while 49 percent gave less than $5.[4]

An effective device used midway in the campaign was the production of a long-playing record containing excerpts from some of Flora's speeches and radio and television interviews given during one month in 1975. The record was presented to all delegates and alternates, as well as to the news media. Additional copies were made available at rallies, for $5 a copy, but workers were careful not to cheapen the campaign by hawking them at meetings. Rather, they could be had for the asking. A film was made at Queen's University, for use on closed-circuit television sets in hospitality suites during the convention.

Encouragements along the campaign trail were many. Wherever Flora went she was received with enthusiasm. Some people travelled many weary miles just to press the hand of this uncluttered woman and say, "Good luck, Flora. God bless you. We're with you."

She offered no spell-binding oratory, but a sincere, straightforward, unapologetic view of the political facts of life, which invariably drew a good press. The fact that she was the one woman among the candidates had its own news value. She refrained from criticizing the other candidates, but ripped into the Trudeau government for its indifference to the concerns of little people.

The populist aspect of her campaign — her obvious concern for the average Canadian pushed around by an unfeeling bureaucracy — was played up by the media. Flora accepted the label Red Tory, but was always careful to define it as a Tory with a social conscience.

Both prior to the campaign and as it progressed, tributes to Flora MacDonald's ability were so many as to be almost embarrassing to one who had not been born to the purple, but had once just been one of six children in a working-class home on the island of Cape Breton.

A month into the campaign she was honoured, along with twenty-four other Ontario women, by the Ontario International Women's Year as one of her province's outstanding women. At a special reception addressed by Premier William Davis, the women were given specially crafted silver and amethyst pins and engraved scrolls.

"You know, it's International Women's Year ... and Flora MacDonald is the obvious answer to twenty million *Why Not* buttons," said a *Montreal Star* writer, who went on to describe Flora's Ottawa office in the West Block as "backstage perhaps to the political career of the century." Flora, she said, "has done very little else in life but slowly, patiently, relentlessly edge her way to power."

A feature writer for *Saturday Night* magazine followed Flora around for a couple of days and said, "Woman or no, she has a chance at the leadership."

"She has class which, by this writer's definition, is primarily grace under stress," said a *Chatelaine* writer.

John Bird, of *The Financial Post*, said that in just a year and a half in Parliament, Flora MacDonald had emerged as a leading national figure and would be a natural for the federal cabinet.

"She is the only Tory who could beat Trudeau and thus save the country from single-party rule and her own party from demoralized decay," said Richard Gwyn of the *Ottawa Journal*.

A *Toronto Star* editorial said, "Miss MacDonald is a politician who helps restore people's faith in politics. . . . Her social conscience is keen — she has plenty of stamina and thrives on hard work. . . . As Conservative leader she would be good for the party and for Canada."

An editorial in *The Globe and Mail* stated: "During the leadership campaign itself, she has shown a capacity for growth — the Flora MacDonald who comes to the end of the campaign trail is better informed, more persuasive and stronger than the Flora MacDonald who began it."

Robert Owen, long-time editor of the Kingston *Whig-Standard*, said: "Flora is a very brilliant person. If she were head of the party it would be, without doubt, the best organized political party. She has an organized mind and insists that other minds are organized too. At the same time, she is a very personable and warm person."

"On technical matters she seeks the advice of experts. Her role as a political leader is to use the best advice she can get to develop policies which respond in a human way to the needs and aspirations of ordinary citizens," said an economist close to government.

"Flora understands the people of this country . . . the problems of our cities . . . the mood of Canadians on an open-book approach to campaign funding and on running a campaign of modest good taste. Her campaign has been run positively and didn't depend on throwing mud at other candidates," said Mayor David Crombie of Toronto.

Political scientists at Queen's University, who had worked closely with Miss MacDonald and retained close contact with her, endorsed her aspiration for leadership and sang her praises. "She's a very acceptable type of woman — neither a strident troublemaker nor a shrinking violet," said Prof. Hugh Thorburn. "She can do anything politically that a man can do, and some things most of them can't do. . . . Her strength is that she has roots in more than one region and has strong national identification through her work in the national party. She would be a good 'broker' between different regional interests."

"She's a progressive, but not a radical," said Prof. John Meisel, who brought her to Queen's. "When I look at the other candidates, she

180

looks better every second." He had his doubts, however, about how much support she would get from "her own kind." As he put it, "Being a woman won't go down well with older women delegates. They can't see a woman in that job."

"Flora's the best of the bunch," said Martin Schiff, a young non-Tory academic, who did some speech-writing for Miss Mac-Donald. "When I went into this [speech-writing] I wasn't so sure Flora had any kind of chance. Now, I'm not so sure she doesn't have the best chance of all."

Tom Sloan, former senior assistant to Robert Stanfield, said: "Her problem will be to get past the first hurdle — the Convention. From then on she will find it simpler to appeal to a much broader spectrum of people."

---

[1] Once in Canadian history, an "uncharismatic Nova Scotian," Robert Borden, had lost three elections and yet had gone on to become a great prime minister. Theoretically, Mr. Stanfield could reconsider stepping down.

[2] As it turned out, four months of campaigning would net him 33 votes.

[3] *The Globe and Mail*, Feb. 13, 1976.

[4] When the leadership campaign was over, Flora was $30,000 in debt. The party came through with half of this, and friends contributed the rest.

33

The war dance begins

No one could seriously fault procedural arrangements for the February 19 to 22 leadership convention in Ottawa. The national committee did its best to narrow the field of serious contenders — going perhaps too far in barring Leonard Jones because he had taken his seat in the Commons as an Independent. The committee distributed delegate lists to candidates, as well as the candidates' policy statements. The hours for hotel hospitality suites were restricted, along with the use of alcohol, so that delegates would have maximum use of reason for the serious business of electing a successor to Mr. Stanfield.

Twelve candidates prepared to offer themselves to about 2,400 voting delegates, which was only one more candidate than in 1967 when Mr. Stanfield gained the leadership. One — Richard Quittenton — withdrew moments before balloting, which left eleven, as in 1967.

Alphabetically, the eleven were Joe Clark, John Fraser, Jim Gillies, Heward Grafftey, Paul Hellyer, Jack Horner, Flora MacDonald, Brian Mulroney, Pat Nowlan, Sinclair Stevens and Claude Wagner. All but Hellyer and Mulroney were members of Parliament.

Hellyer and Wagner were former Liberals. Hellyer had been defeated by Pierre Trudeau in a bid for the Liberal leadership in 1968, and soon after that had been elected to Parliament as a Conservative. In spite of Liberal cabinet experience and prominence as a Conservative, he had been defeated in the 1974 election. Wagner had joined the Conservatives in 1972 and was a member of caucus.

Both men were valued for their experience and made the most of this asset in their campaigns.

Grafftey and Mulroney were lawyers from Quebec — Grafftey with twenty-one years experience in the Commons, Mulroney with none. Flora MacDonald's Ontario rivals were economist and Conservative energy critic Gillies and lawyer and businessman Stevens. The one Maritimer seeking to grasp the brass ring was lawyer Patrick Nowlan from the Annapolis Valley. Western contenders were rancher Horner, lawyer Fraser and the thirty-six-year-old former executive secretary to Bob Stanfield, Joe Clark.

Several candidate organizations bore down on the convention city with expensive wrap-up campaigns. Mulroney was the big spender, putting out large sums for hotel rooms,[1] hospitality suites in five major hotels, lobby decorations and a six-piece brass band. He had hundreds of workers decked out in special jackets and skirts. His giveaway literature was like confetti, only more expensive. He hired the Coliseum, next door to the Civic Centre, for three nights, apparently to keep others from getting it, since he used it for only one night. For that night he was said to have paid singer Ginette Reno $10,000 to belt out a few songs.

Other candidates, including Hellyer, Horner and Wagner spent lavishly, but not in the same grand style. Some of Paul Hellyer's old cronies in Parliament "bought large numbers of drink tickets at 75 cents each and passed them out — thereby at least bending the convention rule against dispensing free alcoholic drinks."[2]

The convention hall on Thursday morning — the opening day of the convention — was literally squirming and bobbing with banners, balloons, mobiles and posters stapled on sticks that could be moved up and down to catch the eye. Delegates were wearing funny hats, badges, lapel buttons, different coloured scarves and even feathers. Elaborate booths were being set up in a corridor on the upper level, and workers at these candidate bases were handing out a variety of come-ons — pamphlets, name buttons, polished apples, fresh-cut daffodils, and invitations to free breakfasts, lunches and dances.

The convention hall was in the last stages of preparation for a media event. At both ends of the auditorium, television networks had their mammoth glassed-in bubbles perched on scaffolding over a section of seating. On the floor, television reporters were scurrying about, wearing telephone headsets and carrying microphones. Two-way radios were bulging out of shirt pockets, and voice pages were now and then going beep in coat pockets. Some media men were hauling backpacks. All were jumping over the electronic cables being snaked down the aisles. A network floor boss, who was asked what he was doing, said, "My primary purpose is to avoid electrocuting myself."

Flora's seating section was noticeable for its absence of overhanging mobiles and balloons. Hers was the one section lacking a banner with the usual giant letters proclaiming the candidate's location; a quality terra-cotta coloured banner was placed there only late in the afternoon. Flora was deliberately downplaying loud display, although there were thousands of stick-mounted Flora signs hidden behind the seats in her section, for use at appropriate times. These had her picture on them in soft brown tones; some signs were larger and showed her with Sir John A. Macdonald. There was just enough mystery about her performance to keep people wondering what she was up to.

Her booth in the upper corridor outside the auditorium was a modest one, compared with others. There were no free apples there, or daffodils, only Flora buttons, free pamphlets and a television set, whose synchronized screen and sound box presented scenes from Flora's life and from her recent leadership campaign. Without saying so in so many words, the low-key approach proclaimed that here was a candidate with a difference.

With pundits in general agreement that up to 60 per cent of delegates were still uncommitted at the beginning of the convention, experts in crowd psychology naturally differ on whether downplay at this stage helped or harmed Flora's final appeal to the delegates. An absence of display when display was the norm could have been interpreted as a weak presence.

At any rate, at the formal introduction of candidates on that opening night, Flora received tumultuous and sustained applause. The usual handclapping was accompanied by unison chanting in her section: "Go, Flora, Go! Flora! Flora! Flora!" By now it was obvious that Flora MacDonald was at the keyboard of a strong organization and was beginning to pull out the stops.

A rousing freedom speech by eighty-year-old former Prime Minister John Diefenbaker, that first night, contained no derogatory reference to Flora. This was a relief to Miss MacDonald and her supporters, who had reason to fear the worst from a man who had painful memories of the last leadership convention and who never seems to forget an injury.

Still, one must conclude that this night of party adulation strengthened the Diefenbaker hero myth. It intensified an emotional identification with Diefenbaker and that section of the party that still resented the Chief's ouster in 1967. This was bound to affect the polls.

Friday's all-day policy sessions were held at the Skyline Hotel. Flora had a hospitality suite there, as well as at three other hotels. In each, a volunteer staff served coffee and home-made cookies — several thousand of the latter — sent up from the MacDonald riding, a hundred miles away.

Flora's organizers and supporters gave her maximum encouragement at each of the four policy sessions. They met her each time at the hotel elevator and conducted her to the assigned ballroom, with the familiar chant, "Go, Flora, Go!" They helped to pack the room and applauded at all the right moments.

The candidate's own performance was superb. She appeared at ease on the podium and read each of her policy statements with feeling and without slavish attachment to the written text. She revealed a fair fluency in passages she read or spoke *ad lib* in French. Her material had substance, and her responses at question time were respectful but animated. There were no cheap putdowns. The general feeling of those who heard the other candidates too was that Miss MacDonald was knowledgeable, astute and articulate.[3]

Her statements — two in the morning and two in the afternoon — contained nothing new; they represented what she had been saying for months across the country, but they were sharpened in phrase and enlivened by wit. A case in point: In a question period, a delegate asked, "Would you take marijuana out of the hands of organized crime and—?" Before he finished his sentence and with a timing that drew applause across the room, she said, "I would take *anything* out of the hands of organized crime!"

At the noon hour break for lunch, delegates were wooed with free hotel meals, paid for by candidates. Hellyer's six hundred guests ordered from a specially printed menu listing New Brunswick fiddleheads, Prince Edward Island potato salad, Newfoundland pickles, Manitoba cole slaw, Ontario boiled eggs, British Columbia salmon, Alberta beef, Quebec ham, Saskatchewan rolls and Nova Scotia apples. Flora, in keeping with her image of the grassroots candidate and her so-far low key campaign, ran a soup kitchen in a nearby church basement. The place was full of customers, who paid

185

The 1976 Conservative
Party leadership convention

25 cents for the modest lunch. The soup was ladled out by Toronto's mayor, David Crombie.

This second day of the convention was topped off with a speech by retiring party leader Robert Stanfield. His swan song came at the end of twenty-seven years in political life, nineteen as the premier of Nova Scotia and eight as federal Opposition Leader.

For a man who had been a peacemaker all his political life, the speech was in character, but it had a boldness often detected in farewell speeches. The speaker could afford to be sharply frank as long as his as-yet undetermined successor wouldn't have to suffer for it. A speech on party unity was not likely to hamstring anybody; and who knows, it might influence some diehards to sheathe their knives.

He said there were enough tensions in the nation, considering its complexities, without Conservatives exaggerating and polarizing party differences. Let the party give itself to reconciling "the aspirations, the hopes and the longings of Canadians in all walks of life and in all parts of our land. That is the way to serve our country. That is the way to beat the Liberals." He went on to say: "This is not the time for old quarrels and feuds within our party. . . . Our party and its mission are more important than the personal likes and dislikes and grudges of any of its members, no matter how eminent." Having done what he could to unite the party, Stanfield said he could turn over the leadership of the party at peace with himself.

Applause lasting more than three minutes brought to an end eight years of a strange relationship. Most people loved Bob Stanfield for his integrity, his competence and his humility, but nearly everybody criticized him because somehow he had never been able to add a glib tongue.

So ended another day. As far as Flora MacDonald was concerned, it had apparently been a success. Flora entertained at a late-evening "hoedown" with a light heart. "Today we accomplished what we set out to do," said her manager, Terry O'Connor. "People are telling us we've built momentum and are sustaining it." He predicted Flora would get about 420 votes on the first ballot, barring a mass switch before Sunday.

The following day — Saturday — would be crucial. Each candidate would have another twenty-minute chance at the delegates. Lots had been drawn to determine the order of speaking. Flora would have number six spot. This would place her after Mulroney and before Hellyer and Wagner — exactly where she wanted to be.

[1] He was forced to give up some rooms to other candidates.

[2] Reported by *The Canadian Press*.

[3] The four themes for all candidates, in the order in which Flora drew her assignments were: (1) Social concerns, (2) Political structures, (3) Resources for tomorrow, and (4) The Canadian economy.

34
The skirl of pipes

As late as Saturday, analysts among the twelve hundred media representatives covering the convention were far from agreeing on what candidates were coming to the top in the pressure cooker, but Flora MacDonald was recognized as among the leading contenders. For the last week she had been placed high by a number of editorial writers, columnists and radio and television commentators.

Christina Newman of *The Globe and Mail* had said that Flora was obviously the "little man's candidate" and the "thinking woman's mentor, the Tory with the most substance, the most sincerity, the toughest mind and the fastest-building strength."

A *Toronto Star* reporter said, however, he was not being deceived by this female candidate's amateur-like organization.

The height of sophistication in politics is to run a slick, professional machine and make it look like an amateur effort by a bunch of happy-go-lucky, low-budget optimists.

That's what Flora MacDonald is achieving. She's had more organizing experience than all other candidates put together. For example, she ran the extraordinarily efficient communication system which helped to win the 1967 convention for Stanfield.

She has a computer in the backroom analyzing delegates' third and fourth ballot preferences, but in the front room, she is serving homebaked cookies and soup, pleading poverty.

All the other candidates put up hundreds of signs. Flora

eschewed signs. The delegates, of course, are all talking about Flora's non-signs, and how she is running an economical campaign.

There had long been speculation, even among Flora's supporters outside of the campaign organizers, about the kind of entrance she would make for her crucial candidate speech. A brass band would have been rather out of keeping with the image she had so far projected. A lone Scottish piper, who had preceded her usual entrances at smaller events, seemed too little for the mammoth occasion. Then came the skirl of pipes — not one pipe but many — and in marched the distinguished Rob Roy Pipe Band from Cobourg and Napanee in eastern Ontario, augmented by additional pipers. It was an emotional moment for the entire house. The pipe band, playing the Skye Boat Song,[1] Flora's favourite Highland air, swept up the aisle with Flora close behind. She stopped off at the platform, and the band continued to the other end of the great hall and out the end doors, still playing. As Douglas Fisher said, Flora and her pipers had a staggering emotional effect to set her on her way.

Then she was launched on her speech:

Ladies and gentlemen, mesdames et messieurs, chers amis.

D'abord, I would like to thank His Worship, David Crombie, Mayor of Toronto, for having done me the honour of placing my name in nomination.

I stand before you today for a very simple reason. I love Canada and I am deeply concerned about its present direction. At the same time, I am confident that I can get us back on the right track.

I've been all over this country and know it from the inside as few others do. And from travelling abroad, talking to leaders of business and government in dozens of foreign countries, I have also seen Canada through others' eyes. These experiences have impressed me all the more with the great natural riches of this land — and with the way Canadians so often take it all for granted.

We are not a boastful people, though once we were. The great Joe Howe a hundred years ago used to say: "Boys, brag about your country," he said. "I do. I brag about all of it. And when they beat me at everything else, I turn on them and say, 'How high do your tides rise?' "

Somehow, particularly recently, we have lost that spirit. The tides of Fundy still rise high, but the tide of public affairs in Canada is at a very low ebb.

Il y a de l'amertume dans le pays. Nous sommes divisés, dressés les uns contre les autres, région contre région, groupe contre groupe.

Le bilinguisme dont nous devrions être si fiers et qui est notre héritage culturel, nous divise au lieu de nous unir. On a tellement défiguré le bilinguisme qu'il est devenu une pomme de discorde entre les Canadiens.

We are distrustful of our government, of our future, of each other. The sense of joyful adventure that once led us to dare to take risks for ourselves, our families and our country is now gone.

In a different era, Winston Churchill put it well. He said: "This nation is descending the stairway which leads to a dark gulf. It is a fine broad stairway at the beginning, but after a bit the carpet ends. A little farther on there are only flagstones, and a little farther on still these break beneath your feet."

The crumbling stones beneath our feet today are inflation, unemployment, social disorder, regional inequities, lack of national purpose. We can't take a leap forward until we secure our footing. Yet I know there is a real yearning to break this cycle of pettiness and meanness of spirit. Canadians want to feel again the joy of daring.

I want to help them do it.

All my life I've been a Conservative, because I share this party's confidence in Canada. I'm a Tory from conviction, not convenience.

Our first leader, Sir John A. Macdonald, whose seat I now represent in Parliament, set our political direction. He showed us the way. Today, as then, ours is the only party that can unite and build this country.

Dans une certaine mesure, notre parti est devenu la victime de la mauvaise humeur qui traverse le pays. Nous aussi, nous sommes devenus peureux et sans audace face à l'avenir. Nous nous sommes repliés sur les alliances traditionnelles et les moyens qui nous ont servis dans le passé. Et cela n'a pas marché.

The old ways don't work for us any more. Unless we as a party rejuvenate ourselves, the people won't respond.

And yet they will respond to something new. They will answer an appeal to get involved. I know, because when I asked for support, I got a response from as many people as contributed to the entire party last year. Now maybe the amounts weren't as big, but the numbers are. What a base to build on! And we need such a base.

Because the first priority of thousands of Canadians I have spoken to recently is to get a new prime minister, they are now looking to the Conservative Party to see what alternative we have to offer. And a real alternative is what we must offer. Not just someone new, but someone who is truly different.

Different in the sense of speaking directly with, not down at, the people. Different in the sense of understanding human needs, not just technical and political convenience, and in the sense of understanding the politics of substance as well as projecting the politics of image.

We need a leader who can attract thousands of ordinary Canadians with their extraordinary strengths. We need someone who will win support on the farms, in the factories, from young and old, and gain respect on the buses as well as in the boardrooms.

As a party we need a leader who has proved the ability to work with others, who can bring all our energies together in an overwhelming onslaught on the malaise of this country and on the divisive deceit of its present government.

I am confident that as leader I can do these things.

I am not a candidate because I am a woman. But I say to you quite frankly that because I am a woman my candidacy helps our party. It shows that in the Conservative Party there are no barriers to anyone who has demonstrated serious intentions and earned the right to be heard. It proves that the leadership of this great party is not for sale to any alliance of the powerful and the few.

Together, you and I and the Canadian people can mobilize a force that will sweep the Liberals from office with a coalition of conviction that nothing will deny.

And once in power we shall do for the country what we've done for the party. We'll give it new life and restore its sense of purpose.

I am confident that as prime minister I can do this. I am confident because my way will be to make you a part of government as never before.

Nous forgerons une veritable honnêteté et un nouvel équilibre dans les rapports entre Ottawa et les provinces. Dans cette confédération, nous cesserons d'obliger les provinces à céder un nombre croissant de leurs responsabilités à un gouvernement central jamais satisfait.

We shall bring to our economy that stability, that certainty, that balanced prosperity we need for genuine growth. And that doesn't mean imposing open-ended controls. We shall help the provinces use the vast resources God gave us to build a second and a third industrial corridor in the West and in the Maritimes. That way we can equalize the prosperity, not just the payments.

We shall use the power of government, not to make government grow, but to help people grow. We won't abuse the power of government, but we shall intervene whenever it is necessary to help regions that are now neglected and people who are truly in want.

We shall make our heritage a source of pride and strength; bolster our Canadian identity; unafraid of foreign domination, foster the many cultures that enrich our society; treasure and respect our linguistic differences. For I am convinced, ladies and gentlemen, chers amis, that the only party that can introduce a sensible policy of bilingualism acceptable to all Canadians is the Progressive Conservative Party. Only we can do it.

We shall straighten out the incredible mess of our assistance programs. In a single stroke we can return independence to those who can work and dignity to those who genuinely need our help.

We shall value excellence. Let's challenge our young, encourage our gifted and reward our most vigorous, for these are the ones who will build this land.

Internationally, we shall return Canada to that position of prestige she once earned. Not for me a policy of gutless compromise. No blackmail price, or no petty commerical gain is worth my country's moral principles or its good name.

And towards the United States, let's act with openness and dignity — and self-assurance. Let's put an end to rancour and discuss our differences without petulance. Let's prove we know the value of our closest friend and ally.

We shall give leadership, through legislation and example, that will bring a new discipline and order to our people and to our streets.

Our armed forces will be given the equipment and the personnel and the backing they need to do the job we ask of them. If I tell our navy to patrol our coasts, I'll give them the fuel to do it.

Ladies and gentlemen, this is the government I want. This is the Canada I want. I come before you with the conviction that this is the government and the Canada that the people of this nation want too.

The goal is ours for the trying — I have committed myself to it. If you share my confidence, if you want this direction for Canada, then join me.

The speech drew strong applause, even from the other candidate sections, and the media proclaimed it among the leading speeches of the convention.

---

[1] The song was written about the original Flora Macdonald and her rescue of Prince Charles.

35
Torpedoed!

Sunday morning — voting day — found Ottawa floundering in the grip of a fresh snowfall, while several thousand Tories rallied to hotel breakfasts to be fed sausage and assurances.

In a Chateau Laurier ballroom, MacDonald supporters were urged by Mr. Hatfield to keep their chins up and keep up the gentle persuasion. "Don't worry one little bit," he said, in effect, "if Flora doesn't do as well as we think she should on the opening ballot. Remember that many of the delegates are firmly committed to another candidate and to a riding association, and they are going to honour that commitment on the first ballot. But we know — we *know* — they're coming to us on the next ballot."

He was passing on, in essence, the findings of surveys of delegates' first, second and third choices. The surveys had been made both before and during the convention. Hatfield didn't say, although he might have done so, that John Robarts ranked third in the first ballot at the Ontario Conservative convention in 1961 and came off a winner.

The New Brunswick premier urged the workers to move in after the first ballot on persons they had cultivated up to that moment. "They'll be emotional, so don't pounce on them. Make it easy for them to come to us."

Flora's manager, Terry O'Connor, was expecting a minimum of 350 votes on the first ballot and hoping for 420. Joe Clark's workers were hoping for about the same number. These two candidates recognized each other as close rivals, and each hoped to get the jump on the opponent on the first ballot and after that to collect from him or her.

By mid-morning the scene had shifted to the Civic Centre. In the almost insufferable heat of the large auditorium, cheerleaders were again urging on supporters in their sections. Bandsmen were leading their musicians in a succession of lively tunes. The assumption seemed to be that the still uncommitted could be won over at the last moment by noise and bobbing signs.

Movable seating on the ground floor level had been cleared away and twenty voting stations set up on the platform side. Each was marked off by guide ropes and with numbers corresponding to a random numbering on delegates' badges. In this way, 140 voters could be channelled between each pair of ropes and checked out on the way to their voting station.

At 12:15, the chairman of the elections committee announced that Dr. Richard Quittenton had withdrawn. The announcement was received without any fuss. The not-unexpected withdrawal left eleven candidates in the race.

The singing of "O Canada" and the offering of an invocation were followed by an announcement that exactly 2,400 qualified voters had confirmed their registration. According to provinces and territories, the breakdown was as follows:

N. W. Territories	8	Ontario	763
Yukon	15	Quebec	603
British Columbia	179	New Brunswick	119
Alberta	212	Nova Scotia	126
Saskatchewan	112	Prince Edward Island	53
Manitoba	132	Newfoundland	78

Looking at these in regional chunks, the west and northwest had 658 voters, Ontario 763, Quebec 603 and the Atlantic provinces 376. Well over 600 of the 2,400 were women.

With delegates preparing to queue up for voting, the final rules were reiterated. Any candidate receiving less than seventy-five votes would be automatically dropped. And when fewer than five candidates remained, the lowest would be eliminated on each ballot. But candidates could choose to drop out after any ballot along the way.

Voting began a few minutes after one o'clock, and for the next six hours the Civic Centre was a house in a hubbub, divided eleven ways

196

against itself in an attempt to find a leader who would put it all together again. Elemental emotions held sway, although always within a set of recognized rules. Only one political animal would emerge from this great bear pit, bearing the teeth marks of the others. To vary the metaphor, the clan was choosing a chief, not on the basis of prowess with the sword, but largely on the basis of reputation and rhetoric.

The last delegates voting on the first ballot hadn't completed voting at 2:10, when Mr. Stevens' brass band blared forth. The performance was slightly out of order but it helped to break the tension.

Results of the ballot were announced in alphabetical order. Rearranged here in descending order, the voting clearly put Wagner in first place, with the rest strung out behind:

Wagner	531
Mulroney	357
Clark	277
Horner	235
Hellyer	231
MacDonald	214
Stevens	182
Fraser	127
Gillies	87
Nowlan	86
Grafftey	33

Flora MacDonald was in sixth place, rather than second or third as she had expected on that ballot. Her 214 votes meant she had received less than 10 per cent of the 2,360 votes cast! What had gone wrong? It was a crushing blow, "a swift and cruel rejection," as the *Financial Post* observed.

By actual count of spotters, 325 delegates had gone to the voting stations either wearing Flora buttons exclusively or with a Flora button in top position among two or more buttons, indicating she was first ballot choice. Some of these voters had obviously faltered with pencil in hand or had been flying false colours. Was it too much for some, at the last minute, that MacDonald was a woman?

197

Hatfield had said: "Don't worry on the first ballot." But Flora had worried. "I had always said if we were to win we had to be ahead of Joe on the first ballot, knowing that either one of us had more potential growth in subsequent ballots than any of the others, but we both couldn't have it." She had been through many political elections and the 1967 leadership election, and she had a feel for those events that other persons with less political savvy sometimes considered uncanny. The Canadian public — she knew she had won that. But the party elite — she couldn't be as sure of that as were her closest workers. In spite of her outward show of optimism — the expected political pose — she had fought back a wave of dread that she just might not make it. Now, the first shock of that reality hit her, like a breaker hurling itself on a headland and falling back. There would be another wave. What would it hold for her future?

Grafftey was out automatically. Gillies with 87 was safe within the ruling, but he chose to drop out. He went and sat with Clark, but not before Stevens beat him to it, in spite of his 182 votes. A stop-Wagner movement had obviously begun, and it was gathering around Clark.

Nowlan, with one vote fewer than Gillies, decided to stay in contention. Hellyer, stunned by his poor showing, concluded he was finished,[1] but he made his move to drop out too late to have it announced before voting began on the next ballot. He made the traditional trek to the candidate of choice — in this case, Wagner — in time to indicate to many of his former supporters where he wanted them to go. His convention arrangements chairman, Walter Baker, went and sat with Clark.

Flora hung on for that second ballot count. When it was announced at 5 o'clock, Wagner still led the pack. His 531 count had moved up to 667. Joe Clark had moved into second place with 532. Mulroney had dropped from second to third place but he had picked up 62 votes for a new total of 419. He was still in contention. Horner had raised his count by 51, for a total of 286, but of course he was finished. Hellyer was already out of the running, so his 118 votes were up for grabs on the third. Nowlan, having dropped to 42 and Fraser to 34 were out on the 75-minimum rule.

Flora MacDonald got a miserable 25 additional votes on the second ballot, bringing her total to 239 and leaving her in fifth place. She could have hung on for one more ballot; but in bottom place, not counting Hellyer, she knew she was finished.[2]

With her heart in her shoes but with her head held high, she left her section and, accompanied by her manager and Hatfield and followed by a band of her delegates, she made the march through a crush of reporters and cameramen, more than half the length of the hall, to Joe Clark's section. Her manager was openly weeping and so were many Flora delegates. The party was met with open embraces. "We'll win together," Joe said. Five minutes later, Heward Graftey joined Clark as well; then came Gillies.

O'Connor said later: "It was the first ballot that crushed us. We had expected 100 more votes, at least — maybe 130. We were dumbfounded. There was dead silence in our box as the fact began to sink in."

The manager and other key workers felt that was the time to move to Clark, but Flora said no; ten thousand people had contributed to her campaign, and her supporters deserved better than that. She was going to stick it out for the second ballot. "So we picked the figure three hundred for our second ballot target. If we didn't get that," O'Connor said, "we decided we would go to Clark. If we got it we'd stay the third ballot, and so on. That was the strategy behind the move to Clark."

The third ballot saw Mulroney drop from 419 to 369, while Clark advanced from 532 to 969 with a gain of 437 votes. Wagner was still in the lead but with a margin of only 34, giving him 1,003.

Mulroney released his delegates to follow their own choice on the fourth and final ballot — the saw-off between Clark and Wagner. The result was close, a 65-vote margin for Joe Clark, giving him 1,187 to Wagner's 1,122. Claude Wagner was gracious in defeat and moved to make the decision unanimous.

As usual, the total vote count had kept diminishing with each ballot, as some delegates chose not to vote at all. In fact, forty of the 2,400 qualifying delegates didn't cast even a first ballot. Only 2,360 voted on the first ballot, 2,337 on the second, 2,341 on the third and 2,309 on the fourth and final ballot — a drop-off on that ballot of 91 qualified voters.

When the new leader, Joe Clark, reached the platform to deliver his acceptance speech, Flora MacDonald, with a radiance reflecting self-respect as well as admiration for a winner, was there among nine defeated candidates ready to shake his hand and launch him on his way.[3] There was no bitterness in her heart. But as the victor brought formalities to an end with a speech stressing unity and dedication to the task of winning the next election, she found it hard to concentrate on the speech. Thoughts of the last four days and of the months of her campaign kept intruding.

1 Hellyer admitted after the convention that he had blown his chances by attacking the "Red Tories" in his Saturday speech. The divisive tactic offended a convention whose mood was for reconciliation of party differences.

2 Gordon Fairweather, MP for Fundy Royal, said potential second ballot supporters backed off when the first ballot was so low.

3 Hellyer had gone home, not realizing, he said, that the defeated candidates would be expected on the platform.

36
Lose a battle...win a war

Post-mortems after sobering events are inevitable, but they can be deceptive if they are too simplistic. One can assign a single cause to a crumpled fender but not to losing an election or going under in a leadership race.

The immediate answer, at the Civic Centre and across the country, to the question "Why?" in Flora MacDonald's case was the obvious one: She was a woman. Robert Jamieson of *The Financial Post* put it as well as anyone: "The idea that Canada may not be ready for a woman prime minister — which is what the exercise is all about — still has too much life in it."

The analysts, from the front-rank members in the MacDonald box at the convention hall to media people across the country, are probably right that being a woman was the *big* thing that lost Flora the leadership. Canada is a follower of sorts, but it may take more than Margaret Thatcher in Britain to set Canada in motion along new lines. The United States, which we tend to imitate more closely, may have to elect a woman president before we are ready to accept a female leader.

Certainly, Flora received no help from her own sex, whatever the reason. The regulations for the appointment of delegates guaranteed at least six hundred women delegates, and they allowed a good many more. If one takes six hundred as the mimimum and, for argument's sake, credits Flora's first ballot 214 votes or second ballot 239 votes to women (which admittedly would be absurd) there were 386 who didn't vote for their fellow woman on the first go and 361 who didn't do so the next time round.

Ontario, as Flora's present province, with 763 votes, male and female, made an even worse showing. Mr. O'Connor's rough calculation for the provinces and territories indicates that about 100 of Flora's 214 first ballot or 239 second ballot votes came from Ontario. Did Ontario withhold the crown simply because Flora is a woman, or were there other reasons? The reasons are probably mixed, as in the case of women's own votes.

It mustn't be forgotten that, in general, the delegates at a party convention are not a cross-section of the rank and file of citizens across the country. They are an elite — better fixed than most, better educated (and proud of it), with interlocking family and business or professional connections. True, one can find a delegate here and there who is outside of these categories, but the point holds: the majority, by far, represent the upper rank of their communities.

Flora knew from the moment of her entry in the race that she could win the country more easily than she could a delegate elite. Read again her comment when she announced her candidacy: "I am a woman. I represent no single region. I'm neither a lawyer, nor a business executive, nor an academic." But she assumed she could, in the crunch, sell herself to a delegate elite as she had obviously sold herself to the general public. It didn't quite come off. For the first time in her life she had experienced what Grattan O'Leary once referred to as "the merciless and inscrutable fortunes of public life."

The elite can be severely faulted for its shallow attitudes. What family status, what connections, could they hint at that would be superior to a proud Highland ancestry or an immediate activist family with both character and principle? What academic education leading to letters after a delegate's name could compare with the education minus letters which Flora had received? And so on. But faulting the elite is one thing. Recognizing its power to put down an invader and in particular an invader who obviously has outclassed it — outclassed it without becoming a snob in the process — is something else.

Another matter: the Red Tory label, in this writer's view, did more to harm Flora than is commonly believed. Flora MacDonald had a problem on her hands when the term first began to be used of her. She could ignore it and hope it would go away, or raise a fuss and call all the more attention to it. Labels tend to be picked up by the opposition and used for whatever purpose they will serve to make points. Politics becomes a dirty game in which insinuations are made.

Flora took still another approach: accept the label but be careful to define or interpret it. "I'm a Red Tory only in the sense that I'm a

Tory with a social conscience, as were a lot of Tories before me." Her career is proof of this social consciousness. It is proof too that, for her, Red Tory was a thousand miles in meaning away from Red socialism. But enemies, or rivals within the party, could still get mileage from the long-established emotional connotations of the term Red.

Delegates who did their own thinking at all knew she wasn't Red in the doctrinaire socialistic sense. Delegates influenced by the label may have steered clear of voting for her just in case there was something in her that they didn't know about.[1]

We're down now to the odds and ends of little reasons, none of which were big enough in themselves to ditch her, but which taken together may have helped.

The mood of Canada at the time this convention was in session was a "law and order" mood — witness the opinion poll that said 74 per cent of Canadian people wanted to retain hanging. The law-and-order candidate, Claude Wagner, received over 1,100 votes, which in itself says something.

Flora's position as an abolitionist was always supported by an explanation of her penal philosophy. She thinks there are better ways of dealing with murderers than killing them, and she would prefer to seek some of those ways. She was never "soft on criminals" as people meant that phrase, but because she wasn't for hanging, people could *say* she was soft on criminals. She wasn't soft on law, but on the contrary said emphatically that Canada's laws should be upheld. But as an abolitionist she was open to insinuations that she was another soft do-gooder. And away went some more votes.

The ghost of Diefenbaker snatched some more, as has already been suggested (page 185).

Always there are inept workers. All the candidates doubtless had some in whom zeal got ahead of knowledge. One of Flora's older workers heard a young Flora enthusiast tell a seasoned Conservative that he was "stupid" if he didn't vote for Flora! The older worker tried to undo the damage, but the Party man wasn't pacified, and for all the worker knew, Flora may have been bad-mouthed for the rest of the day for this one inadvertence. Unfortunately, campaign managers have no way of knowing how many inept workers are turning people away.

A candidate can come up with the odd gaffe herself. A man, as happened on the campaign trail, asks a question about capital punishment. He receives a stock answer but he isn't satisfied. He pursues the matter after the session and gets a "Now let me tell you" lecture. He doesn't like being lectured because, while he doesn't say so, he happens to be the local crown attorney.

These are "little reasons" — unfortunate, but to some extent inevitable. They add up, and sensitive politicians, which Flora MacDonald certainly is, seek to eliminate them the next time round, if those involved in the mistakes have the courage to talk about them.

Anyway, whatever the reason, Flora missed the brass ring. And she knows there's not likely to be a next time. The winner, Joe Clark, is twelve years younger than she is, and he is a very able person. He is, of course, mortal. And besides this, politics is a high-risk occupation at best, and the higher up one goes, the more people are out with their guns. Clark could live to an old age but lose his standing as party leader. It is highly doubtful, however, whether Flora MacDonald in that case would seek the prize a second time.

She has not lost heart. As a member of Parliament she is continuing as if nothing had happened, putting everything into her work as before. Mr. Clark has already recognized her ability, as did Mr. Stanfield, by appointing her to a prominent position and by seating her in the front row of Opposition seats in the Commons.

A federal election could turn out the present Liberal government and replace it with the first Conservative government in fifteen years. Assuming at that time that Flora holds her riding, a reasonable assumption, she would undoubtedly be offered a senior cabinet position. As a CBC analyst said, Flora MacDonald, as a result of the leadership race and her attitude at the convention, has greatly extended her power base. "From now on they come to her."

Flora MacDonald lost a battle. But what is one battle in a long war — a long struggle to help Canada to fulfil its potential among civilized nations? She was confirmed as an important figure in her party — perhaps as the chief spokesman for the best elements of Conservatism in the decade of the 1970s. She has helped to redirect the course of party politics and has revolutionized fund-raising for all Canadian political parties.

Flora lost a battle but she has gained immense respect and admiration. Someone with less sturdy character would have been completely shattered by the rejection of her bid for leadership. It is worth noting that the tears that flowed when Flora was torpedoed were those of her supporters, including men. Flora is tough.

That Flora MacDonald could recover her composure, think of Adlai Stevenson's remark when he lost the presidency — "I'm too old

204

to cry, but it hurts too much to laugh", lead a charge across the convention hall to the operations box of an opponent, pledge him her support and appear later on the platform to welcome him as if nothing had happened is a credit to her, to the spirit of her Highland ancestors who fought with claymores and to the spirit of the now scattered Cape Breton family.

No wonder rival candidates and their supporters crowded into her hospitality suite later that night, proud to shake her hand or kiss her cheek, in recognition that she is a winner.

No wonder several hundred people in her riding gathered to her almost spontaneously, on her return from the convention, to say: "Thank you, we're proud, you're not finished yet."

And no wonder that from all the provinces of Canada and The Territories, over a thousand people showered her with telegrams and letters.[2] The messages, as would have been expected, began with high praise of Flora MacDonald's person and campaign. Many letters contained money toward campaign expenses.

The following comments are representative:

Bravo! While the battle has been won by somebody else, you unquestionably won the war.

You were the Happy Warrior of the convention.

As youngsters in Sunday School, we used to sing, "Fight the good fight with all thy might." This is just what you did, and thousands of those who have followed your campaign are very proud of you.

You have run the race, you have kept the faith.

It takes a great person to win well, and an even greater person to lose well.

The odds against you were far greater than anyone else had to contend with.

How anyone could hold up under that pressure, I'll never know, but you did and I'm proud of you.

You didn't win, but you have made yourself a famous Canadian woman.

As a woman, you were always a lady. As a Tory, you knew your business. As a Canadian of Scottish descent, you showed what Scots gave this country — guts and gallantry.

205

Many of the messages struck out at the classes of delegates which were seen as "doing her in".

You did everything right, and they just weren't ready.

I am sorry, sorry, sorry you didn't win — sorrier that your campaign was rendered bankrupt by unreliable delegates. Where were all the women?

We certainly have a long way to go when women don't even vote for the best candidate and the first woman in the history of Canada to get anywhere near a position of real authority. I grieve not only for you but for my sex and for the whole country as well. . . . I can only say that the democratic process is a very unreliable one and only too often results in the election of second-rate individuals.

It's a pity that women were not loyal enough nor men enlightened enough to recognize the best human choice. Nevertheless you have turned a significant page in the history of Canada.

I am sorry there were so many old maids, male and female, in your party, but I suppose it would be true in any party.

When I heard Barbara Frum announce that the convention felt the country is not ready for a woman, I could hardly credit it. It's not the country; it's those male Archie Bunkers.

In spite of Women's Year (just past), it's still a man's world.

As for the men, all I can say is that they are short-sighted.

You were super! I regret that your party pulled back when the moment of truth arrived.

If, as it is said, the people deserve the leaders they get, and they have turned down openness, honesty, frankness, trustworthiness, ability and patriotic caring such as you had offered them, then, in a sense, they did not deserve the values of statesmanship you so kindly and generously offered them.

When Conservatives have progressed a little further from the caveman . . . philosophy of regarding women as personal servants, a woman may be accepted as an equal.

A letter to an official in the party said: " . . . her placement on the first ballot was the most blatant example of male chauvinism on the part of many of the voting delegates to be publicly seen in this country. . . . Now, the voting delegates have made the job of winning the next election so much harder — and so unnecessarily so! It will be nip and tuck if the Progressive Conservative Party wins the next election. . . . It's becoming increasingly clear to me why the PC Party nearly always sits in opposition."

Another, writing to Flora, said: "Canada is the loser, but had the people of Canada cast the votes I know the results would have been different, because you have proved your real worth from coast to coast."

Many writers of telegrams and letters got beyond striking out at others and talked of positive and lasting results of the MacDonald campaign for leadership.

Ahead of the times, you were, I guess.

You are tomorrow's woman today, a credit to your party and a practical example to young Canadian women.

You have broken new ground for women in politics . . . the time will come when the battle will be less heavily weighted against women.

The spirits of many apathetic and cynical people have been stirred by your recent efforts. You ran a great campaign and made all Canadian women stand a little taller.

So we lost!! But in one way we gained, eh? . . . This world will learn some day just how smart Canadian women are and can be if given the chance.

As a woman, you do credit to all women; as a Canadian you make us glad to be Canadian; as a human being, you give us hope and faith in ourselves; as a politician, you are showing the way to make politics and politicians become respected as never before.

Do not underestimate the boost the success of your career gives to young women when they too encounter trying times.

From now on you are a national leader whose stated opinion on any issue will count for much.

You are known favourably to every Canadian — so now you will be able to mobilize support for those things you believe in.

You are one of the essential ingredients of broadening the base of the party. I urge you to accept speaking engagements throughout the country, to travel as a leader and to adopt as high a profile as your many commitments will allow.

It seems the public needs an adjustment period to realize you truly are the individual we are so desperately seeking to lead our country. Hopefully, this adjustment period will take the form of a senior cabinet position in the next Progressive Conservative government.

This is probably the second step in an important political career — the first step was getting elected. The Conservatives will form the next government, and foremost amongst the policy makers will be Flora MacDonald.

One of Flora's well-wishers' thoughts leaped to the connection between the Canadian Flora MacDonald and the Scottish heroine for whom she was named:

As Dr. Johnson said of your namesake: HER NAME WILL BE MENTIONED IN HISTORY; AND IF COURAGE AND FIDEL-ITY BE VIRTUES, MENTIONED WITH HONOUR.

[1] This view is borne out by a survey of delegate opinion taken by Queen's University political studies professor George Perlin, during the leadership convention; 60 per cent of delegates polled considered themselves "moderates" — neither "right" nor "left."

[2] Added to over two thousand who wrote earlier.

Bibliography

AIKEN, GORDON, *The Backbencher* (Toronto: McClelland and Stewart, 1974).

AITCHISON, edited by J. H., *The Political Process in Canada* (University of Toronto Press, 1963).

BOUGUET, MICHAEL, *No Gallant Ship: Studies in Maritime and Local History* (London: Hollis and Caret Limited, 1959).

BROWN, GEORGE W. and ALLEN S. MERRITT, *Canadians and Their Government* (Toronto: J. M. Dent & Sons, 1971).

CANADA, GOVERNMENT OF, *Federalism for the Future* (Ottawa: The Constitutional Conference, 1968).

COURSE, A. G., *Windjammers of the Horn, Story of the last British Fleet of the Square-rigged Sailing Ships* (London: The Trinity Press, 1969).

COURTNEY, JOHN C., *The Selection of National Party Leaders in Canada* (Toronto: Macmillan, 1973).

DEMPSON, PETER, *Assignment Ottawa* (Toronto: General Publishing Co. Ltd., 1968).

DOERN, G. BRUCE and PETER AUCOIN, eds., *The Structures of Policy-making in Canada* (Toronto: Macmillan, 1971).

DUGAN, JAMES, *The Great Iron Ship* (New York, Harper and Brother, 1953).

GORDON, WALTER L., *A Choice for Canada* (Toronto: McClelland and Stewart Ltd., 1966).

HALIBURTON, E. D., *My Years With Stanfield* (Windsor, Nova Scotia: Lancelot Press, 1972).

HARVEY, E. ROY, *Sydney, Nova Scotia, an Urban Study* (Toronto, Clark Irwin, 1971).

HULME, KATHRYN, *Annie's Captain* (Toronto: Little, Brown and Company, 1961).

IREMONGER, LUCILLE, *The Fiery Chariot* (London: Secker & Warburg, 1970).

JACKSON, ELVA E., *Cape Breton and the Jackson Kith and Kin* (Windsor, N. S.; Lancelot Press, 1971).

——, *Windows on the Past* (Windsor, N.S.: Lancelot Press Ltd., 1974).

KIPLING, RUDYARD, *Rudyard Kipling's Verse* (Toronto: Copp Clark, 1919).

KORNBERG, ALLAN, *Canadian Legislative Behavior* (Holt, Rinehart and Winston, Inc., 1967).

KRUHLAK, OREST, RICHARD SHULTZ and SIDNEY POBIHUSHCHY, eds., *The Canadian Political Process* (Toronto: Holt, Rinehart and Winston, 1970).

LOCKHART, J. G., *Strange Tales of the Seven Seas* (London: Philip Allan and Co., 1929).

MacMECHAN, ARCHIBALD, *The Book of Ultima Thule* (Toronto: McClelland and Stewart, 1927).

————, *There Go the Ships* (Toronto: McClelland and Stewart, 1928).

MANTHORPE, JONATHAN, *The Power and the Tories* (Toronto: Macmillan of Canada, 1974).

MEISEL, JOHN, *Working Papers on Canadian Politics* (Montreal: McGill-Queen's University Press, 1972).

NEWMAN, PETER C., *Renegade in Power* (Toronto: McClelland and Stewart Ltd., 1963)

————, *The Distemper of our Times* (Toronto, McClelland and Stewart, Ltd., 1968).

PARKER, JOHN. P., *Cape Breton Ships and Men* (Toronto: George J. McLeod Limited, dist. 1967).

————, *Sails of the Maritimes* (Aylesbury: Hazell Watson and Viney Ltd., 1960).

PARKS, M. G., ed., *Western and Eastern Rambles: Travel Sketches of Nova Scotia, Joseph Howe* (Toronto: University of Toronto Press, 1973).

PATTERSON, GEORGE, *A History of the County of Pictou, Nova Scotia* (Montreal: Dawson Brothers, 1877).

PORTER, JOHN, ed., *Canadian Social Structure* (Toronto: McClelland and Stewart, 1967).

PREBBLE, JOHN, *The Highland Clearances* (Harmondsworth, Eng., Penguin Books, 1963).

RUSSELL, PETER, ed., *Nationalism in Canada* (Toronto: McGraw-Hill Co. of Canada Ltd., 1966).

SCHWARTZ, MILDRED A., *Public Opinion and Canadian Identity* (University of California Press, 1967).

SHERWOOD, ROLAND H., *Pictou Pioneers* (Windsor, N.S.: Lancelot Press, 1973).

SPICER, STANLEY T., *Masters of Sail: The Era of Square-rigged Vessels in the Maritime Provinces* (Toronto: Ryerson Press, 1968).

STAEBLER, EDNA, *Cape Breton Harbor* (Toronto: McClelland and Stewart Limited, 1972).

STEWART, WALTER, *Shrug* (Toronto: new press, 1971).

————, *Divide and Con: Canadian Politics at Work* (Toronto: New Press, 1973).

STEVENS, GEOFFREY, *Stanfield* (Toronto: McClelland and Stewart, 1973).

TAYLOR, CHARLES, *The Pattern of Politics* (Toronto: McClelland and Stewart, 1970).

THORBURN, HUGH G., ed., *Party Politics in Canada* (Scarborough, Ontario; Prentice-Hall of Canada, 1972).

VINING, ELIZABETH GRAY, *Flora, A Biography* (Philadelphia, J. B. Lippincott Company, 1966).

WALLACE, FREDERICK WILLIAM, *In the Wake of the Wind Ships* (Toronto, Musson Book Company Limited, 1927).

————, *Wooden Ships and Iron Men,* (Boston: C.E. Lauriat, 1937).

WALWORTH, ARTHUR, *Cape Breton, Isle of Romance* (Toronto: Longmans, Green and Co., 1948).

210

Index

214

Set in 10/12 Baskerville
Printed on 60 lb. Commercial Text
1 2 3 4 5   Alg   80 79 78 77 76